Group Sales

for Arts & Entertainment

Group Sales

for Arts & Entertainment

The Myths
The Markets
The Methods

TREVOR O'DONNELL
with BOB HOFMANN

EntertainmentPro
an imprint of
Quite Specific Media Group Ltd.
Hollywood

First Published 2005
© Trevor O'Donnell and Bob Hofmann

ISBN 0-89676-254-8

Quite Specific Media Group Ltd.
7373 Pyramid Place
Hollywood, CA 90046-1312
V: (323) 851-5797 F: (323) 851-5798
info@quitespecificmedia.com
www.quitespecificmedia.com

Imprints: Costume & Fashion Press, Drama Publishers,
By Design Press, EntertainmentPro, Jade Rabbit

Book design: Sally Blakemore
Arty Projects Studio, Ltd., Santa Fe, NM
Typography and Production Coordination:
Jeffrey Cohen

Table of Contents

Part I: The Myths

Part II: The Markets

Part III: The Methods

Who Should Read This Book?

This book is primarily about volume ticket sales for stage entertainment with an emphasis on Broadway, touring Broadway shows, and regional producers and presenters of musicals, plays, and other forms of popular arts and entertainment. The process of selling group tickets is the same for nearly all forms of live entertainment, however, so the information presented here will be meaningful to performing arts centers, arenas, concert venues, circuses, fairs, festivals, and providers of various forms of fixed-site arts, culture, and recreational activity. We sincerely hope that everyone in the arts and live entertainment industry who benefits from group sales income or deals with group sales as a part of his or her job will find this book enlightening, informative, and useful.

The book is primarily intended for industry leaders, policy makers, marketers, operations managers, and group sales supervisors who need a clearer understanding of what group sales is and how it works. It begins with a detailed critique of inefficient industry practices, continues with a breakdown of volume ticket markets, and concludes with a useful set of recommendations for helping group sales practitioners enhance productivity.

Not everyone will want to read every part of this book. The first part was written specifically for producers and executive leaders. The second and third parts contain information that is relevant to those who design and execute marketing and sales programs. Knowing that most readers will pick and choose, we have approached certain points from multiple perspectives and stressed others with deliberate reiteration. Thorough readers who feel they are covering familiar territory are more than welcome to skip ahead.

It is no secret that group sales is somewhat of a mystery to most people in the arts and live entertainment business. We as an industry don't really like group sales and most of us don't seek careers in this field, much less desire to specialize in selling bulk ticket inventory. If someone had told Bob or me fifteen years ago that we'd be writing the industry's first book on group sales, we'd have been horrified! Bob comes from a directing and producing background and I come from a performance and marketing background. Group sales? Yuck! This was definitely not part of our original entertainment industry ambitions. But it is where our careers took us—actually, Bob dragged me into it—and original intentions not withstanding, we wound up being surprisingly successful at it.

We do recognize that most of our colleagues have not been pulled in the same direction and that group sales isn't a priority for folks pursuing more glamorous careers. And, yes, it is understandable that many of our colleagues want to preserve their distance from group sales. But this is an industry that is entirely dependent on ticket sales, and when well-meaning professionals who disdain group sales find themselves in management positions that require a solid understanding of how ticket revenue is generated, neither the distance nor the ignorance can be easily excused.

Group sales professionals drive tens of millions of dollars in ticket sales throughout North America every year despite being managed by an industry that is largely unaware of what they do or what kinds of customers they serve. This book will demonstrate that the current group sales yield for stage entertainment is low compared to what it should be and that the collective unwillingness to master group sales is preventing the industry from capitalizing on substantial untapped potential.

So, then, who should read this book?

PRODUCERS

Producers have the most to gain from maximizing revenue but they have too much to do to conduct an in-depth study of the group sales process. Those producers who devote a couple of hours to reading this book, however, will have much of the information they need to make highly profitable strategic decisions about marketing and *selling* their ticket inventory.

GENERAL MANAGERS

General managers make most of the policy decisions that govern how tickets are sold, but few general managers have hands-on experience with group sales. Most are dependent on the advice they receive from box office treasurers, marketing managers, and occasionally, group sales staff. This book will arm general managers with a "big picture" perspective so they will be able to interpret the advice they receive and introduce profitable changes in a discipline where "that's the way we've always done it" is often the primary strategic consideration.

PRESENTERS

Presenters are struggling with diminishing subscription audiences, hard-to-motivate baby boomers, and emerging consumer markets that are not predisposed to attend live performance events. Group sales, especially in regional markets, is ripe territory for audience development but presenters don't always have the necessary tools to capture new volume ticket markets. Those who read this book will discover lucrative new sources of volume ticket sales and will have a clearer picture of what must be done to make group sales a more productive generator of new audiences and incremental revenue.

THEATRE OWNERS

Theatre owners and venue managers, especially those who run their own group sales operations, will naturally garner substantial rewards from enhanced sales. This book will help theatre owners understand how outdated industry standards and decades-old box office "traditions" stand in the way of attracting new audiences and productive new sources of long-term, sustainable ticket revenue.

MARKETING DIRECTORS/MANAGERS

"Sales" is likely to emerge as a major trend in the coming years, and marketers will soon find themselves dealing with complex new business-to-business partners who were once relegated to the group sales category. This book will highlight some long-neglected opportunities for partnerships to lower costs, carry the marketing message to remote consumers, deliver measurable results, *and* physically deliver ticket holders to the theatre's doorstep. What more could a marketer ask?

AD AGENCIES

Ad agency writers and designers who are called upon to create group sales materials often lack information about what motivates individuals who buy volume tickets. Thus, they end up simply changing the phone numbers on materials that were created for different purposes. This book will provide useful information to agency creative teams so they can create meaningful group sales tools for carefully targeted volume markets.

GROUP SALES DIRECTORS/MANAGERS/STAFF

Group sales staffers are charged with a nearly impossible mission: "Go out and get new group customers but never forget that group sales is one of our lowest priorities." This book will give salespeople powerful tools for capturing new markets, and it will give them powerful arguments for changing the way this industry approaches and serves group buyers.

BOX OFFICE TREASURERS

The business-to-consumer (B-to-C) model that has governed box office operations for decades is changing in profound ways. This book will identify new sources of volume ticket sales in the business-to-business (B-to-B) sector, and it will give box office treasurers the information they need to develop productive service standards and new systems for capturing sales from B-to-B sources.

TICKETING PROFESSIONALS

The business-to-consumer model that has dominated ticketing for decades has blinded many ticketing professionals to significant sources of volume ticket revenue. It has also placed unnecessary burdens on ticket-buying business people whose potential can't be realized within the B-to-C model. Understanding the distinction between B-to-C and B-to-B revenue sources will help ticketers modify their business models for increased profitability.

PERFORMING ARTS PROFESSIONALS

Opera? Dance? Shakespeare? Classical music? This book deals mostly with popular entertainment but the principles, markets, and methods outlined here are perfectly relevant to performing arts disciplines that cater to more narrowly defined audiences.

STUDENTS

It is disturbing but true that young professionals in performing arts and entertainment will need to find new audiences and sources of incremental revenue if they plan to have careers in the field. This book points to lucrative new markets, business oriented solutions, and innovative responses to rapidly changing market conditions. Few readers will come to this book better prepared than students who haven't fallen prone to the that's-the-way-we've-always-done-it school of management.

SMALLER THEATRES AND
COMMUNITY-BASED ARTS ORGANIZATIONS

This book deals primarily with larger arts and entertainment providers, but it also contains information for organizations that rely on smaller, more consumer-driven local markets for group business. Not all of the information in this book will apply to smaller organizations but the underlying concepts are applicable to most group sales situations.

THE UNINFORMED AND EMBARRASSED

There are plenty of seasoned veterans in the stage entertainment industry who will confess—in private—to a certain amount of ignorance where group sales is concerned. This book will give these poor souls an opportunity to steal away and learn in secret so they may return to their conference rooms and say with authority: "I'm concerned that we're not penetrating the MICE sector. Let's ask our DMO to get us a list of DMCs so we can find out if we're maximizing our relationships with MPI, SITE, and ASAE. Maybe we need an enhanced presence at the Motivation Show or EIBTM next year."

TRANSLATION:

"I'm concerned that we're not penetrating the meetings, incentive travel, conventions and events sector. Let's ask our destination marketing organization (usually the convention and visitors bureau) to get us a list of destination management companies (local companies that plan business gatherings for remote clients) so we can find out if we're maximizing our relationships with Meeting Professionals International, Society of Incentive Travel Executives and American Society of Association Executives. Maybe we need an enhanced presence at the Motivation Show (a trade event for the incentive industry) or European Incentive and Business Travel Marketplace next year (another trade event for incentive travel buyers)."

The Blind Men, The Elephant, and Group Sales

In an ancient parable in which several blind men are introduced to an elephant, each is asked to experience a portion of the elephant and form a perception based on the characteristics he has discovered. The one who feels the leg thinks the elephant is like a tree; the one who feels the tusk thinks it is like a spear; the side, like a mountain; the tail, like a rope; the ear, like leather. When they begin to compare notes, however, the men argue vehemently because none has the necessary perspective to assemble the parts into an understandable whole.

When it comes to group sales, we in the stage entertainment industry are like the blind men and the elephant. We come at group sales from distinct perspectives and few of us have the breadth of experience necessary to describe the whole beast. Sadly, we remain committed to our limited points of view, and rather than step back to view the big picture, we cling to our respective parts and hold them up as evidence that we have all the information we need to understand group sales. Then we argue incessantly without getting anywhere:

"Group sales is a pain in the ass."
"Group sales is too much busywork for my staff."
"Group sales is the foundation that keeps us in business."
"Group sales is a front for dubious resellers."
"Group sales is all about bus tours."
"Group sales is little old ladies and unruly kids."
"Group sales is my livelihood."
"Group sales is the future."
"Group sales is the past."
"Group sales is a necessary evil."
"Group sales is a nuisance."
"Group sales is corporations and businesses."
"Group sales is travel and tourism."
"Group sales is dying."
"Group sales is thriving."
"Group sales is expensive."
"Group sales is more trouble than it's worth."
"Group sales is an untapped goldmine."

Everyone can "prove" that his or her perspective is accurate by pointing to concrete evidence, but no one can sway others with a comprehensive picture of how the diverse parts work in concert.

This book is an attempt—by people who may have seen more of the elephant than anyone else—to describe group sales. Our goal is to help the industry see the big picture and, in so doing, understand that this gentle giant is far more good-natured, appealing, and useful than any of us imagined.

PART I

THE MYTHS

The fact that group sales happens at all is a bit of a miracle. Ours is an industry with a curious set of misperceptions about the process and about the people who buy the tickets.

Here are several myths that determine how we approach group sales and why we fail to capture its full potential.

Groups Are There To Fill the Seats You Can't Sell to the *Real* Customers.

In the mid 1980s Bob and I worked together in the marketing department of the Pittsburgh Public Theatre. There we learned a valuable lesson about the hierarchy of theater audiences, a hierarchy we used then—and most of us use now—to prioritize our marketing efforts.

First came the subscribers. They were the dependable core, the ultimate priority, the lifeblood of the American regional theatre. After all, Danny Newman told us this was true in his book *Subscribe Now!* and we all embraced it as gospel.

Next came the single-ticket buyers, the necessary, if somewhat less predictable, patrons on whom theatres have been depending for centuries. Shakespeare flew the flag over the Globe and single-ticket-buying Londoners came from far and wide. With minor modifications it was the same in Pittsburgh in the 1980s, and to a surprising extent, it is the same today: tell the world about the show and wait for people to buy tickets.

Finally there were the groups, those gently yielding seniors and students whom we asked to fill the ring of seats around the edges—the seats you couldn't sell to the first- and second-priority customers. As we fretted over the marketing campaigns and season seating maps, groups were amorphous blobs of undifferentiated, unsophisticated seat fillers who could be poured into the horseshoe around the sides and rear like so much lime chiffon Jell-O® into a holiday ring mold.

Made perfect sense to us. Made perfect sense to everyone. The theatre industry accepted this as a fundamental truth and handed it down like ancient lore: the seats face the stage, the lights shine on the performers, the telemarketers call at dinnertime and the groups are there to fill the seats you can't sell to real customers. Amen.

But the problem is, it isn't true. That's not what groups are at all. It's not what they're for; it's not how they work; it's not how they see themselves; and it is definitely not how they like to be treated. This assumption that we all take for granted—an assumption that goes to the core of *what we think we know* about our audience—is just plain wrong and astonishingly counterproductive.

The following chapters will describe other myths but this is the foundation myth that underlies them all. This is the root of the problem, the core misperception from which all others arise, the great earth-is-flat understanding that limits our horizons to what we can or perhaps want to see with our own eyes.

It is the myth the live entertainment industry clings to with unquestioning faith, and it is the myth that blinds us to productive new markets worth tens of millions of dollars in incremental sales.

Group Sales Is About Selling Tickets to Consumers.

Forty years ago group tickets were mostly purchased by consumers: social group organizers, charity fundraisers, senior group leaders, and teachers. They were essentially local consumers who happened to be buying in bulk for their friends, peers, and students. These consumers were motivated to organize entertainment outings for their "groups," so they ended up coming to us with requests for volume purchases.

The shows and venues liked the idea of selling more consumer inventory to volume buyers so they made some adjustments and established a modified box office operation (advance reservations with deferred payments) for processing group ticket orders. Gradually these systems became the group sales business model that most of us use today. The unique needs and expectations of these consumers determined the structure of the systems, and as long as the buyers remained the same, everything worked just fine.

Now, however, the ranks of buyers have swelled and the volume ticketing system that was built for consumers is carrying the weight of commercial traffic it was never designed to handle.
Like an old two-lane bridge that groans under the weight of heavy trucks, our infrastructure is out of date and incapable of meeting new demands. Contrary to prevailing perceptions, group sales is not a steady flow of little old ladies and schoolteachers. Rather, it is a fluctuating cycle of heavy and light demand from diverse commercial and consumer market segments. Sometimes the demand is so intense that traffic backs up badly on this rickety old bridge causing much of the commercial traffic to take different routes to more user-friendly destinations.

To put it simply, some of our best business customers won't put up with our outdated mom-and-pop consumer methods so they bypass us for more accessible products.

If we hope to capitalize on the demand from these markets, we're going to have to evaluate the systems that were put in place for consumer groups back in the 1960s and 1970s and then think about designing new infrastructures for meeting the demand that our new business-to-business (B-to-B) markets have to deliver.

But before we start designing new infrastructures, we'll need to know exactly who these customers are and what they need from us so we will be able to give them the services they require.

Here is a general breakdown of the types of B-to-B ticket buyers whom our old consumer infrastructure is trying—but often failing—to serve. These buyers represent clearly definable submarkets, each with its own needs, motivations, expectations, and methods of operation. What distinguishes them from traditional consumer customers is that they are business people and professionals who buy entertainment for different reasons.

Legitimate companies that buy tickets to re-sell to others for profit such as tour operators, vacation packagers, and travel-related service providers.

In the retail world, middlemen like these are seen as valuable wholesale partners who sell products to remote or otherwise unreachable consumers. In our industry, they can become the means to ensure that groups in Berlin or Tokyo or Toronto or Baton Rouge or Dubuque or the town down the road can buy tickets to our shows when they book with their local travel professional or tour operator. Wholesaling is a new idea in live entertainment, however, so we don't fully embrace these selling partners, many of which can represent extraordinary incremental potential.

Businesses that acquire entertainment tickets as a part of the services they provide to other businesses, such as destination management companies, meeting planners, event planners, and incentive travel companies.

There is a large and active industry made up of companies that plan, coordinate, and manage meetings, conventions, events, and incentive travel for other businesses, corporations, and associations. Among the people who work for these companies are professionals who book pre- and post-show parties or secure blocks of tickets to hot shows for post-meeting entertainment. Our consumer-based service standards can make it extremely difficult for these high-end B-to-B clients to access our tickets, so they often produce their own in-house entertainment or seek out entertainment that is easier to access.

Organizations that use entertainment tickets to leverage donations and/or reinforce affinity, such as charities and membership organizations.

Any organization that thrives on donors or members needs to add value to their affinity relationship by hosting gala fundraising events, finding reasons to bring them together for communal activities, or giving them exclusive entertainment opportunities. Gala organizers, membership directors and association leaders know that hot tickets can fetch healthy returns for their worthy cause or give members an attractive reason to stay involved. Smart group sales people know that affinity markets are excellent sources of high volume business. And smart producers of national tours are beginning to recognize that large national affinity organizations can support touring shows with enormous volume ticket purchases in multiple markets.

Corporations and businesses that use entertainment tickets to entertain clients or motivate employees.

There is no simple way to characterize the corporate and business markets for group sales because the individual buyers differ from one business to the next and the motivations change depending on who is buying the tickets and for whom. In general, we know that tickets to hot shows are given as incentives to workers or used as a stimulus to improve morale. We also know that businesses use tickets to entertain clients. Every good group sales database will include numerous local businesses that are excellent sources of high volume, top-dollar repeat sales. But these businesses need consistent access to our products with professional service standards that reflect their own methods of operation.

Companies that use entertainment tickets to leverage their competitive edge or increase their own group business, such as local attractions, hotels, restaurants, and service providers in the venue's vicinity.

The largest untapped market for group sales in the stage entertainment industry may be found among businesses, attractions and service providers that cater to group clientele. Arts and entertainment venues have a history of "go it alone" when it comes to group sales; we sell our tickets and seldom think about how our sales activity relates to other local businesses. But ask the volume ticket buyers and they'll gladly tell you that group outings are *destination events* that require multiple package components, including transportation, food, accommodations, shopping, and other leisure, educational or cultural activities. Partnering to form package products is a hot trend in group sales and stands to open large productive new markets for community-minded entertainment providers. But this partnering takes a collaborative sensibility rather than the competitive, sometimes even defensive, attitude that has governed our approach for decades.

Paid professionals who book group entertainment tickets as a function of their jobs, such as educators, community activity coordinators, geriatric recreation directors and student activity directors.

Our consumer-based service standards seldom take into account the fact that many of our customers work for businesses, educational institutions, government bodies, and community organizations that have various reasons for obtaining tickets and have diverse business practices that dictate when and how they can buy. Unlike consumers who have a fair amount of flexibility, business buyers come to us with extraordinary constraints that make it impossible for them to respond as their consumer counterparts do. Professional buyers need professional service standards and dynamic partnerships that recognize, respect, and conform to the ways their businesses function. Otherwise, they book only when they can or they simply don't book at all.

Individuals who earn incentives for booking group entertainment, such as group travel planners and entrepreneurial group leaders.

I once met a woman at a senior group leader event in Massachusetts who regularly bought group products for her church, her senior center, her bridge club, and her apartment complex. When she wasn't buying and selling group travel and entertainment packages, she was taking cruises, motor coach tours and luxury fly-drive vacations—all for free! Many of the people we call group leaders are enterprising entrepreneurs who earn valuable incentives for their organizational efforts. These group travel planners are quasi-professionals who expect to be recognized and rewarded for their considerable influence on where and how the group dollars are spent.

These business and professional buyers are a huge boon to the stage entertainment industry, and in an era of diminishing subscriptions and distracted single-ticket buyers, they represent markets with significant growth potential. But their productivity is seriously diminished by the fact that our business model is built entirely on the needs and expectations of consumers, not businesses.

These business markets have clients who are literally begging for access to our products but who can't adjust their own business infrastructures to accommodate our B-to-C methods. Our reluctance to understand the clientele, to know how they do business, and to make our business model fit theirs is preventing us from capturing significant new sources of B-to-B sales, which could represent huge new audiences worth tens of millions of dollars in incremental revenue.

WARNING

To anyone who has ever used the term *group leaders* to refer to their entire universe of group buyers, here is a friendly little warning. In the professional group sales arena, *group leader* refers only to one narrow category of buyer, typically a senior group activity coordinator, a senior group travel planner, or a senior consumer who books on behalf of his or her peers. Group leaders don't have to be seniors but enough of them are to give the name a specific connotation.

Using *group leader* as a generic label for your customers sends a clear message to your most important clients that you don't understand the markets with which you do business. It is also potentially offensive to clients who are not group leaders and who prefer not to be labeled as such.

Better to use the words *group buyers* or *volume ticket clients* instead. Look closely at the revenue these individuals deliver and you might even opt for *best customers*.

Bulk Is Beneath Us.

Here is a little one-act play about a myth:

"The More You Want, The Less You Get"
An Absurdist Tragedy in One Scene

It is three days before opening night and the theatre's lobby bar is out of liquor. The facility manager calls the distributor.

FACILITY MANAGER: Hi, I need to order two cases each of top shelf gin, vodka, scotch, and bourbon.

DISTRIBUTOR: Great. Let me fax your order to our stock department, and I'll get back to you in two or three days to let you know if we have any.

FACILITY MANAGER: Have any? Three days? I can't wait that long. And what if you don't have any in three days?

DISTRIBUTOR: I'm sorry. We can only move as fast as our stock department, and they take three days. I can tell you that we don't have any top shelf product left. We don't usually sell that by the case anyway. We're bound to have some bottom shelf brands, though. You'll love it. You bulk buyers always go for the cheap stuff.

FACILITY MANAGER: But that's ridiculous! I have a business to run. My customers are depending on me. They want quality and they expect service!

DISTRIBUTOR: Sir, you are simply ordering too much, and people who buy too much have to wait. That's the way it works. Now you'll have to excuse me. I have a long line of good customers who have the taste, discretion, and money to ask for quality products one bottle at a time and I really need to get back to them.

FACILITY MANAGER: But this is ridiculous. I'm one of your best customers! I spend thousands of dollars with your company every year. You act like you don't want my business. (click) Hello? Hello?

CURTAIN

This reads like an exaggeration, but it isn't. Make it about tickets to live stage events and it is a conversation that happens daily in group sales offices all over North America. Legitimate businesses that serve discerning customers want to buy our best products in bulk, but our policies, procedures and standards of service are often inadequate if not outright insulting to them.

Typically the only people who know about these conversations are the folks answering the phones in the group sales department. These customer service reps hear the complaints of the bulk buyers. They hear the indignation from customers who want to buy thousands of tickets in advance but can't because of punitive deposit policies. They hear the complaints of the tour operators, who buy more tickets than any other customers and spend tens, sometimes hundreds of thousands of dollars, but are still being treated as third-class citizens. They hear the would-be customers saying over and over again, "If you can't give me the service I deserve as a volume buyer,

I'll spend my money elsewhere." Or, worse, "Do you have any idea how many more tickets I would buy if you were willing to work *with* me instead of *against* me?"

If high volume B-to-B customers fail to maximize their potential with us or walk the other way, something is terribly wrong. If we fail to capture new business from promising new volume customers—bulk buyers who are banging at our doors asking for access—something is broken and needs fixing.

There isn't a venue in North America that can afford to turn away sales but it is done all the time because of an attitude that says to volume ticket buyers, "We're not interested in your business."

Groups Buy Tickets.

Groups do not buy tickets; individuals buy tickets in bulk on behalf of groups.

This seems to be an obvious point, but it demands scrutiny because we don't think in terms of individual decision makers when we market to groups. We think instead of generic collectives of blind sheep whose individual motivations have been surrendered to an overriding group will. We attribute few, if any, singular impulses to group purchasers, and we assume that their collective decisions are driven by tastes and expectations that conform to the lowest common denominator.

When we do this, we craft impotent sales and marketing messages that speak to nobody and we make strategic decisions rooted in vague, misguided notions about the buyers we're targeting and what motivates them to buy. In short, when we think about groups as if they are groups, we market to groups and groups don't buy tickets.

But if we take time to identify the *individuals* who buy tickets in volume, we can isolate different kinds of buyers and learn what motivates them to make their purchasing decisions. We can take our comparatively short lists of group buyers, break them out by buyer type, prioritize them, and target, with an extraordinary degree of specificity, the ones who are responsible for the most sales.

Then we can sit down and talk to them!

The entertainment industry loves expensive focus group research. We pay research companies to assemble sample groups of single-ticket buyers and grill them about their buying habits hoping that these twelve strangers truly speak for our target demographics. Then we use this general information to go out and market more persuasively—we hope—to the rest of the ticket-buying public.

Ironically, we can call twelve of our largest group ticket buyers any time we want, invite them to lunch, ask them pointed questions, and learn *exactly* why they buy tickets, how they buy tickets, how many they buy, and what we can do to get them to buy more. We can ask them about their customers and benefit from decades of in-depth, first-hand, professional knowledge about the consumer group markets they serve. We can ask them to comment on the products and services we offer so we can learn how to serve them more productively and how to make our sales relationships with them more mutually successful.

Then we can take all these findings, apply them to the rest of our group clientele, and know with certainty that we've understood their motivations and addressed their individual needs. And we can do it all for the cost of a couple of lunches. There are plenty of loyal group customers who would be thrilled to sit down with us and discuss how we can forge more productive alliances and how, together, as business partners, we can make sure the volume markets for our tickets continue to grow.

This odd disconnect between the entertainment industry and its volume ticket buyers is so pervasive that industry leaders—producers and presenters who have multi-million dollar interests in the success of their group sales—don't always know who's buying what or whether their customers' full buying potential is being realized. And in markets with independent group sales agencies, where the sales process is even further removed, shows, presenters, and producers have no contact whatsoever with their volume customers.

Not long ago I attended a group sales presentation hosted by a large regional presenter. At the post-show party in the lobby I ran into an old client, a tour operator whose business was located in a large city some sixty miles from this particular venue. This tour operator bought hundreds of tickets from the theatre's group sales office every year and ran scores of bus tours to its shows. Her purchase volume was so large that her company easily qualified as the theatre's single largest and most important customer. At the reception, she and I spoke to various theatre staffers, including the group sales director, the marketing VP, the general manager, and eventually the CEO, but not one of them knew who she was. They didn't know her, her company, how many tickets she bought, how many remote consumers she had delivered to the theatre or how many thousands of dollars she had contributed to the theatre coffers over the last few years. Here was an individual whose personal buying decisions made her the theatre's single most influential sales partner, yet she had no connection with the people who benefited from her long-time patronage.

Anyone who has sold a candy bar for the school band or a box of cookies for her Girl Scout troop has heard the old saw "know your customer." It is a tired cliché but it contains some wisdom for an industry that, although frustrated by group sales, is unwilling to know, understand, or learn from its most productive patrons. In many ways the answers to our group sales problems lie in closing the communication gap that exists between industry leaders and the individuals who make volume purchase decisions. All it takes is a willingness to see the buyers for who they are, understand how they do business and enter into relationships with them that embrace them as valuable partners. It also takes some friendly, personal inter-action from time to time and a willingness to recognize and reward them for being our best customers.

If, on the other hand, we continue to treat the individuals behind group purchases as generic nonentities, we shouldn't be sur-prised if they don't hear what we have to say.

Try this:

Ask your group sales director to give you the names of your organization's top five buyers along with the number of tickets they bought in the last three years and the total dollar value those purchases represented. Go over the names with your group sales director then ask him or her to schedule a lunch meeting with each buyer—on you, of course.

At lunch, after you've thanked these folks for their support, ask them why they buy your tickets, how they use them, and to what extent they've been successful. Ask them what it is like to buy group tickets from your organization and how it compares with buying products and services from other suppliers. Then ask them if there is anything you can do to help them buy more tickets.

Encourage them to be honest with you. Pay close attention to what they say. Are they telling you something that might help you help them buy and sell more tickets?

One Size Fits All.

Here's a real myth:

Ancient Greek legend has it that an evil landowner called Procrustes once forced travelers who crossed his property to stay in his home and sleep in a bed that either stretched or sliced them to a uniform size. Naturally, most of his visitors suffered or died in the process. From this comes the expression "Procrustean bed," a name we give to things that demand conformity at an enormous or ridiculous cost.

With that in mind, think about these four volume ticket buyers:

CUSTOMER A is a corporate party planner for a major multi-national electronics company. He plans parties for anywhere from five hundred to one thousand people in major markets across North America. The corporation he works for prefers to host pre- or post-show parties in conjunction with blockbuster entertainment events and wants to be able to book them in advance for cities across the country through one central source. The approximate value of this gross annual business is six hundred and fifty thousand dollars.

CUSTOMER B is a day-trip tour operator in a population center eighty miles from one of the country's top regional entertainment markets. She can deliver four to eight buses per week to a reasonably popular show, but she needs to plan six to ten months in advance without having to invest too much cash too far in advance and she needs complete information on all scheduled performances (whether or not they're on sale to local consumers). The approximate value of this gross annual business is two hundred thousand dollars.

CUSTOMER C is a popular theme restaurant located near a major entertainment venue in a large midwestern city. The group sales director there wants to sell dinner/show packages to her own database of group buyers, and she's willing to assume responsibility for both selling and booking the tickets because it will drive incremental group dining business for her. Her restaurant is part of a franchise of similar restaurants with locations in most major markets. They are among North America's most aggressive marketers of group dining. The approximate gross value of this annual business is seventy-five thousand dollars. (A tour producer who negotiated a national deal with this chain might realize more than one million dollars.)

CUSTOMER D is an old gal at Pinecrest Senior Village who always puts together the outings for the choir. She's a real go-getter and her nephew works at the bus company so she always gets a rate there. She books about thirty-five to forty inexpensive tickets for one show every year. The approximate gross value of this annual business is one thousand five hundred dollars.

Guess which customer the current group sales business model is designed to accommodate. No, it's not the top dollar corporate client or the high volume tour operator or the sophisticated marketing partner. It's our dear old friend at Pinecrest, bless her heart.

Believe it or not A, B, and C are real customers. A finds it incredible that he's ready to buy hundreds of top price tickets worth tens of thousands of dollars but can't get anyone to take his calls. B has learned through years of indifferent service that it is easier to sell the dinner theatre down the road. After all, they treat her like gold because she delivers so much business. C is ready to rock and roll but needs a level of service that reflects her volume potential, the value of her proprietary database, and her willingness to do all that proactive outbound sales work.

But D knows the ropes. She has grown accustomed to the bad service and onerous payment policies. She's not picky about seats because she buys the cheaper ones and they're never that good anyway. She's OK with the advance payment because it's not that much for the lower-priced seats, although she usually has to write a personal check. And, hey, she's retired so she's got all the time in the world to get through the booking process.

The live entertainment industry is lucky to have a lot of customers like D who are delivering serious business. But they are part of a diminishing market that shows few signs of being replenished. The ranks of senior group leaders and their followers are thinning and the next generation doesn't seem to be interested in the same kinds of group activity. If we continue to invest our energies in seniors, we'll find ourselves trying to court senior baby boomers who prefer independent activity, who don't have time to muck around with complicated ordering, and who don't necessarily want to go to shows on buses with a bunch of *old people!*

Group behavior changes from generation to generation just as subscriptions and ticket-buying activity do. Senior groups are going the way of subscribers, and if we're not prepared, we'll be watching group numbers go down without knowing why or how to bring them back up. In many markets, this is already happening.

Customers A, B, and C are ready to do business with us, but *they simply won't bother if we insist on treating them like Customer D.* They buy a lot of goods and services from a lot of other suppliers, and they're accustomed to being treated like VIPs who spend a lot of money. In most industries people who spend a lot of money do get VIP treatment because they deserve it. If our industry treats them all like frugal retirees we can't be surprised if they have nothing to do with us.

When we force our diverse B-to-B customers into a Procrustean bed of inflexible sales policies, we fail to capture incremental revenue from promising new sources. In many cases we offend the customers we should be working hardest to accommodate.

Try this:

Sort your group sales database into buyer types (see next section for breakdowns). Take a look at the relative diversity of the buyers on your list.

Do the bulk of your buyers fall into one or two categories? Which categories are they?

If there is a noticeable lack of diversity, is it because of the nature of your available buyers? If you have mostly senior group leaders and schools, is it because these are the only buyers out there?

Or is it possible that your markets are defined not by who out there is willing to buy, but rather by the limitations you place on access to your products? In other words, is it mostly group leaders and schools because those are the only buyer types who can work within your present system?

Are there buyers out there who are willing to buy but who are unable because you've been using outdated systems and inappropriate policies? Has this narrow focus prevented other types of potential buyers from accessing your products?

Ask your group sales staff to track inquiries that *don't turn into sales*. Knowing why some interested customers don't buy tickets can be a lot more revealing than knowing why others do buy.

Group Buyers Are Parasites.

Here's a true story that illustrates a contemporary myth:

Not long ago a successful Broadway producer and his management team had gathered for a meeting at which one of the top execs made a startling observation. Tour operators, he said, were a bunch of unscrupulous scalpers who weren't to be trusted. Some of those gathered in the room gave a wry chuckle as if a dirty secret had just been revealed. Others nodded in agreement. The rest of the room silently absorbed the wisdom of this show biz veteran. Another fundamental truth in theatre lore had just been reaffirmed by the most powerful people in the business.

Later during that same meeting the subject of Broadway's suffering group sales came up, and despite much hand wringing and teeth gnashing, not a person in the room had a clue how to solve the problem. These seasoned business leaders who had so cavalierly dismissed their biggest customers moments earlier were speechless and ill equipped to understand, let alone respond to, a failing market that normally delivers fifteen to twenty percent of their sales.

Somehow along the way we've allowed ourselves to believe that many of our group customers are parasites or dubious resellers.

We've developed a suspicion that the service we've been so generously offering to sweet old ladies and school kids has been infiltrated by shadowy commercial interests. These *for-profit* businesses have been sneaking in the back door of group sales and taking advantage of discounts that were meant for group leaders and teachers. Travel companies have been buying tickets at a reduced rate and reselling them to consumers—*just so they can make money*. The nerve!

This bias in our industry causes us to question the legitimacy of many of our most valuable customers. It is understandable that we harbor such suspicions given the traditional consumer orientation of our model and our industry-wide ignorance about the types of businesses group buyers represent. And, to be fair, there have been instances in which less-than-honorable brokers have sneaked in the group door masquerading as legitimate travel industry buyers—not a lot, but just enough to cast a shadow of suspicion on the rest.

But the overwhelming majority of business buyers represent legitimate companies that want access to bulk inventory at a price that rewards their volume potential. These companies are accustomed to buying bulk products from suppliers who bend over backward to earn and keep their business. They buy hotel rooms and airline seats and dinners and cruises and sightseeing tours and admissions to all sorts of attractions—all from companies that appreciate them because they deliver sales in such volume. These buyers are accustomed to working with *supplier partners* who value their long-term business, their distribution channels, and their willingness to deliver customers to their partners' doorsteps.

When they come to us, though, we treat them like foxes in the henhouse.

In an era of diminishing consumer markets, B-to-B volume markets represent significant growth potential. If we want to tap into this potential, we're going to have to pay close attention to who is buying our tickets, how their businesses work, and what we can do to work with them in the most productive manner. When we do, we will discover lucrative new sales and marketing partners—valuable wholesalers—who are eager to help us expand the market for our products.

If we continue to give them only the most begrudging service and then castigate them behind closed doors, we'll have no hope of maximizing their full potential.

Think about this:

There is a similarity between the hospitality and stage entertainment industries that may be instructive: both sell the right to occupy a small piece of real estate for a limited period of time. For us it's seats; for them it's rooms. We're both dealing with perishable inventory—seats and rooms lose value if not sold by a certain time—and we have a mix of consumer, trade, and group clientele.

The two industries differ in their approach to moving their inventory, however. Stage entertainment usually employs PR and marketing to inform local consumers about shows, hoping that these consumers will be motivated enough to purchase tickets.

Hospitality, on the other hand, uses sales to establish relationships with third party wholesalers. These wholesalers deliver remote consumers in exchange for priority access and price incentives, such as commissions, net rates (volume rates that enable them to mark up a price without overcharging the consumer), or graduated pricing (the more you buy, the lower the price).

The hospitality and live entertainment business cultures are determined to some extent by the proximity of their markets—entertainment markets are mostly local whereas hospitality markets, made up of travelers, are remote. These divisions are becoming less clear every day, though. Stage entertainment is becoming increasingly dependent on remote markets, especially in destination cities, and group sales is beginning to recognize that wholesalers and B-to-B clients are their most promising new sources of incremental revenue.

Live entertainment professionals may find that a close examination of the hospitality model will help them capture emerging B-to-B markets without having to reinvent the wheel.

They'll Call Back.

A few days after I started working in the group sales department of a large western presenting theatre, I noticed a sudden lull in phone activity. When I mentioned to my sales manager that it was unusually quiet, she said, "Oh, we put the answering machine on so the staff could take lunches and catch up on paperwork."

To some readers this won't come as a surprise—it is common practice in group sales offices everywhere. We are, after all, the best entertainment product in town and the customers who really want tickets generally do call back. Besides, we have convenient recorded messages that tell them where to fax their orders or what details to leave so we can help them when we do eventually connect.

Others will recognize this as a business horror story, and they're right. People who sell to groups in more professional settings know that any single phone call can represent thousands of dollars in sales. They know that it costs money to get people to call, that many make the call on impulse, that competition for group entertainment dollars is stiff, and that the most promising buyers are business people who expect a businesslike response. They also know that even if most buyers do call back, *many of them do not*, and failing to take every single call that comes in during business hours is like throwing money out the window.

The fact is that we as an industry offer fairly dismal service to volume ticket buyers. Here is a list of some of the worst offenses:

We hold our high volume customers at arm's length, preferring to deal with them only through low-level staffers, under-supported group departments, or outside agents.

In many organizations, group sales sits either at the bottom of the organizational hierarchy or is farmed out to independent agents who control local customer databases. The salespeople who interact with the volume ticket buyers are usually so far removed from their superiors that they receive few top-down service imperatives, and they have little, if any, bottom-up influence on policy. The result is that the best customers often get the poorest service and nobody realizes it is happening. Or worse, they know it's happening but they don't understand what it costs in terms of lost revenue and unrealized audience growth.

We condescend to group customers assuming that anyone who would travel in a group is beneath our dignity.

This is especially prevalent in the theatre where entertainment professionals who have backgrounds in *"performing arts"* look down their noses at tourists and people who arrive at the theatre on buses as if their money is less valuable or they are somehow less deserving of access to our shows. I once worked with a marketer in a large presenting/producing organization who, in the midst of a presentation on developing new volume ticket markets, slammed her fists against the conference table and screamed, "Why on earth would we want to sell tickets to tourists?" (The answer to which, of course, was because we have empty seats in every house!) It was as if tourists were less deserving than people who lived nearby. This attitude was a perfect example of the bias that can underlie the myths. These biases, rooted as they are in genuine artistic or communal impulses, are understandable but they are tremendously counterproductive.

We create defensive, sometimes even punitive, group sales policies for mega-hit shows then leave the policies in place when we're desperately trying to encourage group business.

New hit shows sometimes need to regulate group sales to keep a suitable balance between group and single-ticket volume. Unfortunately, the temporary guidelines these shows put in place to *moderate* access can become fixed policies that don't change when demand is less intense. Some of these unnecessarily restrictive policies have been embraced as convenient excuses for avoiding the work it takes to maximize sales. "Sorry, there's nothing I can do. That's the policy." If the ultimate criterion for evaluating group sales policies was "What will help us sell the most tickets?" most of these old policies would fail the test. One might think that in a multi-million dollar discipline like group sales that these outdated policies would be rare, but they are all too common.

We allow arcane operational clauses in box office agreements to prevent rather than nurture business.

In some contracts the word *traditional* is used in such a way that box office personnel can say, "That's not how it has been done *traditionally* so you can't ask us to change the way we do it now." No matter how productive it may be to introduce new standards of service or new operational procedures, and no matter how much the markets for our products may change, traditions have a refuge in contract language that codifies that's-the-way-we've-always-done-it attitudes and operational behaviors.

We plan consumer-based on-sale strategies that make it impossible for businesses to buy our tickets.

Group markets are not so fluid as we think. Most group buyers are constrained by schedules and calendars that dictate when and how they can plan group activities. We tend to ignore these constraints, however, and plan on-sale strategies (when the tickets go on sale, in what quantities and to which target markets) as if groups are just sitting by their mailboxes waiting for us to tell them when they can see our shows. A sit-down (long-running engagement) of a large Broadway tour opened recently in a popular U.S. visitor destination, and even though the show was planned to run for almost a year, groups were front-loaded (forced into a limited number of early performances) to "keep pressure" on the early inventory. Of course the only group buyers who could plan for such a narrow window of opportunity were the comparatively flexible local consumer groups, so millions of dollars of B-to-B potential was lost and single-ticket sales had to pick up the slack.

We treat all group buyers as if they were little old ladies even if they run sophisticated businesses or buy top-dollar tickets for large corporations.

Our treatment of group buyers has been mentioned already—and will be mentioned again—but it bears repeating. Bob and I have spent the last fifteen years traveling around the world talking to buyers who'd say, "I'd love to buy your tickets but my company can't do business with your industry the way you're set up. You want me to buy volume tickets but you treat me like some third class citizen." This refrain has been repeated so often and in so many forms by so many buyers that it has become one of those absurd realities that you learn to accept: The more tickets a customer wants, the less likely he or she is to get them.

We staff our group sales operations with industry insiders instead of trained group sales professionals.

All too often group sales interaction consists of show business insiders talking down to would-be buyers. I once inherited an employee in a group sales office who fancied himself an artist and deeply resented his work in the groups department. His customer interaction was a mix of bitter sarcasm and rigid policy enforcement that said in essence to buyers, "If I'm going to be forced to deal with you people, you're going to have to play by the rules." In an ideal situation, the best group sales people side with the customers and work hard to get them what they want despite the myriad policies and procedures that stand in their way. Most stage entertainment salespeople, however, side with the shows, venues, or producers and raise policies as defensive shields against the barbarian hordes.

In many cases we treat buyers as if they're lucky to be getting seats at all and refuse to extend common sense services to stimulate increased ticket sales.

I've worked in several theatres where incoming group sales volume was measured in inches rather than tickets or dollars. The inches referred to the thickness of the pile of orders that accumulated beside the fax machine while group sales processing staff were engaged in other activity. Days and sometimes weeks would go by before the orders were confirmed, but we always had a relative, if inexact, measure of pending group order volume. (For those of you who are scratching your heads in disbelief, this is actually true and surprisingly common—even in some of the largest U.S. markets.) Meanwhile the customers who are trying to spend thousands of dollars putting together complicated group activities wonder where their orders are. Or they've moved on to other, more responsive products. In any other business capturing volume purchases would be a top priority, while in ours it ends up being a when-we-get-around-to-it chore.

In short, we as an industry maintain service standards that barely mask our disregard for volume ticket buyers. Then we sit in conference rooms planning strategies, fretting over sales, and quietly cursing those damned groups for being so hard to motivate.

What makes this situation so ironic is that extending excellent customer service to group buyers is inexpensive, relatively easy to implement and by far the most effective way to sell more tickets. The year we instituted a no-call-goes-unanswered policy at the theatre mentioned above, we broke every group sales record in the theatre's history. It was a no-cost change that allowed us to capture an extraordinary amount of new business.

It doesn't cost anything to embrace our customers and thank them for their patronage. It doesn't cost much to revise our service standards to make them more helpful or user-friendly. It doesn't take much time or energy to update outmoded box office procedures or plan workable on-sale strategies or take time to learn what clients need rather than telling them what they can get. Reaching out to our best customers, recognizing them as selling partners, and treating them like respected business colleagues may cost us a bundle in humility, but it's a small price to pay.

But even if we're determined to swallow our pride and embrace volume buyers, we must keep in mind that the impetus to give excellent customer service cannot come from the bottom of our organizations. We can't expect the new person who answers phones in the group sales office to do it alone. We can't expect the group sales manager or the group sales director or box office treasurer or even the vice president of marketing to do it. It must be an organization-wide imperative that grows out of a true understanding of, and appreciation for, the customers who buy our products. We are going to have to face this issue as an industry, address it from the top, filter the changes throughout the individual organizations, and fix the problems where they occur. We can't hope to offer truly productive customer service if we don't know our customers, if we distrust our customers, if we dislike our customers, or if we don't value them enough to recognize them and reward them for their patronage.

When we allow our prejudices toward groups to excuse bad service, we risk overlooking the simplest and most cost-effective ways to develop new sources of volume ticket sales.

Try this:

Here's a simple exercise to assess the service standards your organization employs:

Imagine you are the senior vice president of sales at a large local business and you've decided to take your top-producing sales executives and their families to see a hot new show. Think seriously for a minute: you are a high-level corporate professional and you've decided to allocate several thousand dollars from your limited incentive budget to dangle a really "nice" incentive in front of your best salespeople—and "nice" in your world means good seats on a popular night with a quality dinner before the show.

Now, go through the process of getting those tickets. Yes, actually do it. Look up the number you need to call, call the number, talk to the staffer, place your order, and take it through to the point where you have to commit. (Obviously, if your voice will be recognized, you'll need a surrogate to do the calling.) See for yourself what a sophisticated buyer who wants to spend serious money has to do to get group tickets to your show.

Did you get through to someone? Were you given the service you deserved as a buyer who wanted quality and service? Did you get the deferential service that should be available to a senior executive who wants to buy several thousand dollars worth of tickets in one phone call?

How would you rate your organization's ability to serve a customer like this?

What kind of long-term business would you expect from this type of buyer given the service you received?

Marketing to Groups Means Changing the Phone Number in the Brochure.

The practice of marketing to *groups* rather than to *individual* volume buyers is nowhere more apparent than in the ads and printed materials we disseminate. Advertising agencies are adept at crafting media messages for single-ticket-buying consumers, and they have a certain facility with direct mail, but few of the writers and designers at these agencies are armed with an in-depth understanding of what motivates group purchases.

Sending consumer brochures to group buyers simply doesn't make sense. It assumes that volume ticket buyers are entirely pre-motivated and that they are prepared to make all sorts of inferences about the show, about its appeal to their groups, and about the extent to which it will support the needs and expectations of numerous single-ticket-buying group members. It also assumes that group buyers will be able to sell the show to their constituents using abstract logo art and coy, superficial promotional copy.

In addition to knowing whether the show will appeal to their groups, the individuals who buy group tickets need to know *why it is in their interest as volume ticket buyers* to book the show. They need language that speaks to them as individuals who book on behalf of others and they need clear, specific, descriptive copy they can use to inform and motivate their constituents. Group buyers are salespeople. They need appropriate sales tools to do their jobs, and they need to understand how they will benefit if they do the job well.

If we want effective ads and collateral (printed promotional materials) for group sales, we must write and design materials to educate and persuade the decision makers who book advance tickets. They need answers to the questions that will be uppermost in their minds:

- What *exactly* is this show about? What is the *story?*
  How do I describe that story to the rest of my people?
  Where can I get a concise paragraph that describes the show in clear, upbeat, persuasive language?

- How are we going to feel when we sit in those seats watching it?

- Will anyone complain? Is it offensive or controversial?
  Is it appropriate for all members of my organization?
  Is it good for a business gathering? A social gathering?
  A religious gathering?

- What are the key selling points?

- What is my incentive as the person who books the volume tickets?

- Will I have access to marketing materials so I can promote my group event(s)?

- Is this ordering process going to be difficult or time-consuming?

- What other amenities are available near your venue for my group event?

- Do the available performance dates fit in with my organizational calendar?

- Can I order online?

- Must I order and distribute the tickets or can I let my people order individually?

- What are the prices? Will my company make money? Can I pass on savings to my group? Will this price work in my package? Are there any value-added extras? Will my boss approve this purchase?

- Where can I find a nearby restaurant? Hotel? Transportation? Other attractions and entertainment for my itinerary? Are there resources available that will help me package your show to make it more marketable to my customers?

- What is the venue neighborhood like? Is it safe? Is it convenient? Can we park a bus? Does the driver get to see the show, too?

- Does the venue have an elevator? Are there stairs? Handicapped seating? How far do my customers have to walk?

- Will I get an extra ticket for the escort?

- How does this show fit as a part of what it means to visit the venue neighborhood?

- What else can you give me that will help me market your show to my people?

- Who is my contact? Will I be ordering from the venue? What is this ordering process going to be like? Will I have access to the information I need? Availability? Seats? Flexible payment deadlines?

Once, while working on a West Coast tour of a reasonably popular Broadway show, I was asked to help craft some collateral for a Southern California group mailer. The ad agency that was writing and designing the piece kept refusing to use the customer-oriented copy points that I had outlined and insisted on the generic single-ticket copy ("But that's the way we've always done it!"). So I visited the web sites of all New York's independent group sales agents to see what sort of copy *they* were using to sell the Broadway production of this show.

Each group sales agency had completely rewritten the ad agency's consumer copy to address concerns that were common to their group buyers. It was astonishing how large the gap was between what the ad agency had provided and what the sales agents had created to fill the information void. Unfortunately, the group agents didn't have access to professional copywriters, so the writing was not uniformly excellent and the show was not as well marketed as it might have been.

It doesn't cost any more to write and design effective group sales materials. All it takes is a willingness to understand how group buyers differ from single-ticket buyers and the effort to speak to them in language that is meaningful, informative, and above all, persuasive.

When we assume that group buyers respond to generic consumer enticements, we fail to acknowledge the role they play as extensions of our sales and marketing teams. But if we give them the tools they need, they'll be properly motivated and sufficiently informed to book and resell the show in the most effective manner.

Try this:

Imagine there is a tour operator in a city who's just outside your local media market. He has a lot of money tied up in motor coaches and needs to keep the buses rolling to stay profitable so he's always looking for an interesting new package to sell to his database of loyal group customers. (Remember, his customers aren't getting your media messages because they are outside of your local market.)

Today a promotional brochure arrives in this tour operator's mail—it's the group sales collateral you just approved for your next show.

How good a job does this piece of mail do in convincing this business owner that your show is worth selling? Is he convinced? Is this show worth his investment in time and resources to create and promote a new package? Does it answer all of his questions? Does it suggest what else might be included in the package to make it more marketable? Does it give him the tools he needs to sell the show to customers who aren't getting the information anywhere else? Does it help him understand how a package centered on this show will fare next to the other seventy-five day-trip packages he sells? Does it indicate whether such a package will be profitable to his business?

How much extra work will this potential buyer of several thousand dollars worth of show tickets have to do to fill in the information your mailer failed to address? Will he do it?

Could you have sent him something more persuasive? Something that met his needs in a more effective manner? Something that made him say, "Wow. I can't wait to start promoting this to my customers!"

The Play's the Thing.

We take great satisfaction in knowing that when people come to our shows their primary motivation is the performance we're selling. They decide to come to the show because it's the show they want to see and everything else is secondary. If they dine at a nearby restaurant, it's because they're going to the show. If they take a cab or secure some form of transportation, it's because they're going to the show. If they shop or spend the night or enjoy some other attraction in the venue neighborhood, that's great, but their reason for coming to the neighborhood is the show. For most consumers, the show is the reason for the outing and all other activities are secondary considerations.

But for an awful lot of group buyers the play isn't necessarily the thing. For them the *package* is the thing, and even if the package is centered on the play, the components that come with it can make or break the sale.

Group entertainment events simply don't happen without at least three package components: tickets, transportation, and some sort of pre- or post-show dining. Some group trips contain multiple package components including hotels and other forms of entertainment to fill multi-day itineraries. For others still, the show may just be an added diversion in an extended event that was organized for an entirely separate reason such as a convention, a multi-day tour, a shopping adventure (yes, there are tours just for shopping), a student trip to an educational music festival, or a regional corporate business meeting.

It is extremely important for sellers of group entertainment to understand that tickets alone do not always meet the needs or expectations of the group buyer. Many group buyers are faced with a multitude of options for their group activity, and because they are busy people, they'll often choose the one that makes their job easiest.

Here's an illustration that is based on very real discussions with interested buyers:

A young group sales director for a major midwestern entertainment venue is at a Meeting Professionals International (MPI) convention talking to a potential customer:

SELLER: Hi, I noticed your association was planning an event in our city next spring. We have an extraordinary new show scheduled for those dates and I think it would be a great way to add entertainment to your gathering.

MEETING PLANNER: That sounds interesting. I'd need a lot of tickets. Maybe fifteen hundred to two thousand.

SELLER (heart pounding): No problem. We're not on sale yet so we can block an entire house for you and make it an exclusive event for your convention.

MEETING PLANNER: Okay, now I'd need a venue for a pre-show reception and it would have to have a sound system because we'd need to do a presentation. Food is an issue, too, as is transportation from the convention center. Also, I can't get involved in ticket distribution so I'd need a way for my delegates to book themselves. Can you help with that?

SELLER: Well, we just do the group tickets and you'd have to buy them all at once. I'm not sure where you'd go for all the other stuff. But I'll be happy to send you a contract.

MEETING PLANNER: I've got a few options to consider closer to the convention site. Thanks, anyway.

SELLER: But the show is really great. You'd really love it.

MEETING PLANNER: I know, but there's a lot I'd have to do and I don't have time to pull something like that together.

Now try that again, but this time imagine the seller is ready to help fill up the rest of the package:

MEETING PLANNER: Okay, now I'd need a venue for a pre-show reception and it would have to have a sound system because we'd need to do a presentation. Food is an issue, too, as is transportation from the convention center. Also, I can't get involved in ticket distribution so I'd need a way for my delegates to book themselves. Can you help with that?

SELLER: Oh, that's easy. There's a new museum directly across the street with a fabulous party space that can accommodate up to two thousand with comprehensive AV support. The sales director is a colleague of mine who is here at the conference; I'll make sure to introduce you to her. They do in-house catering but they don't have an exclusive so you can bring in someone from outside if you prefer. Here's a list of great caterers. We always work with Fresh Connection and I think they're the best. I'll have the owner drop you an email. Now as for ticketing, we have a few interesting options. We have a service that can accommodate single-ticket sales at a modest service fee so with the group price break and the four dollar per ticket fee, you're still coming in under the regular box office price. That should be an easy sell for your delegates and you won't have to do anything more than promote the event and give them our web address. And I know the best motor coach charter service in town for getting everyone to the theatre. They buy a lot of tickets from us and they're terrific. I'll send you that contact, too. Sounds like an incredible party. And it looks like we can cover all your needs in short order.

BUYER: Wow. That sounds great. I've been looking at a lot of options but this one seems like a real winner. Can we plan a conference call for next week?

SELLER (beaming): No problem. I look forward to it.

Notice that the seller didn't have to do the package work. All she had to do was make sure the buyer had the necessary package resources. Because she understood the buyer's needs and because she had the strategic relationships necessary to make referrals, she made the buyer's job easy and, thus, closed the sale.

When group ticket sellers fail to see the big picture from the perspective of the buyers, they miss opportunities to meet those buyers' needs in productive ways. We need to understand that our shows are only part of what we're selling; the more we can offer to complete the package, the more customers we will serve and the more tickets we will sell.

The play may well be the thing, but as any gift giver knows, some things are a lot more attractive when they're wrapped up in a nice package.

Test your package potential:

How does your venue's neighborhood measure up as a group destination? Here's a little quiz:

- Name three restaurants within a half-mile radius of your venue that can accommodate a group of fifty.

- Identify the three spaces closest to your venue that can be used for pre- or post-show parties or receptions.

- Name three caterers that can service those party venues.

- Name the three nearest hotels that accommodate mid-range and high-end groups.

- Where do buses park at your venue? How far away? What is the cost? Can drivers park and lock or do they have to sit with the equipment?

- How are groups welcomed when they arrive at your venue? Is the experience the same for a Cub Scout troop, a high-end fund-raising gala, and a top-dollar corporate group?

- If you were creating a group package that included a show at your venue, what other things in the neighborhood would you put on the itinerary for a day trip? A two-day trip? A weeklong convention?

- Name five attractions or service providers in your vicinity that cater to group buyers. Identify them as either competitors or potential package partners.

- What are the names printed on the sides of the buses that drop people at your venue most often? Who runs those companies? Do they rent buses or sell package tours? What other packages do they sell and how does yours compare?

A group-dependent organization should have all these answers at hand with plenty of details to support them. Selling your show means selling your destination and selling your destination means selling packages.

How competitive is your package?

Sales is About Sending Flyers and Answering Calls.

Traditionally, group sales in the entertainment industry has been a *reactive* process: we send mailers or place ads and wait for the phone to ring. In most markets what passes for group "sales" is largely phone answering and order processing of inbound calls.

In a few major markets, however, over the past ten years, group sales has become a fiercely competitive process where producers, venue owners and sales agents reach out to prospective buyers *proactively* and court them with direct, persuasive, in-person sales messages. The ones who do it most effectively take time to learn the buyers' businesses and establish meaningful personal and political relationships within the business communities that deliver the most sales. The ones who bring new sources of volume sales—and thus new audiences—into American theatres and entertainment venues are creating bold new collaborative relationships with strategic partners in non-traditional business environments.

In the early 1990s Cameron Mackintosh created a small sales organization called Theatre Direct International (TDI) to market and sell group tickets for his New York productions of *Les Misérables*, *The Phantom of the Opera*, and *Miss Saigon*. As a producer of musicals in London—a major tourism market—he knew that Broadway was doing comparatively little to tap the tourism industry. So he developed TDI and charged its managers with a uniquely proactive mission: go find travel industry buyers and sell them tickets.

Within ten years that imperative opened numerous new target markets, including, but by no means limited to, travel and tourism; businesses and corporations; meetings, events and destination management; international wholesale travel; hospitality; education; and a whole range of traditional and non-traditional consumer group and single-ticket buyers. TDI built creative infrastructures for serving B-to-B buyers and generated many millions of dollars in Broadway ticket sales. It was the product of hard work and no small amount of tenacity, but at its core was a fundamental shift in the prevailing attitude toward sales. That small go-find imperative launched an *outbound* sales movement that changed the way Broadway did business with volume ticket buyers.

There is an enormous difference between the go-find school of thought and the pick-up-the-phone-if-it-rings philosophy that once governed sales in New York and still governs group sales in many North American markets. The go-finders have discovered significant untapped potential, and they've found that developing and serving new volume ticket markets—especially among B-to-B buyers—is extremely rewarding. Meanwhile, the pick-up-the-phone-if-it-rings crowd is learning that powerful demographic changes in traditional group markets and intense competition for group dollars from competitors can be threatening if not altogether fatal.

Sales must be an active rather than a passive process, one that involves targeting desirable markets and engaging in outbound, in-person, direct sales activity. The days of sitting in the office answering calls are over. A well-trained customer service rep (CSR) can do that. Group sales professionals have to go out into the markets they serve, find the people who should be buying tickets in bulk, convince them to buy, and then find ways to serve them. The attendant task is to make sure that the venue or show is prepared to serve the unique needs of these new clients. Yes, it'll be more expensive; and, yes, changing the infrastructure will be challenging, but the increased yield will more than cover the cost of putting another CSR on the phones.

Sales is a proactive, persuasive, outbound, assertive, creative, strategic endeavor. Everything else is operations.

Try this:

Work with your senior group salesperson to create a simple pie chart that identifies what percent of his/her total work hours is devoted to the following:

- Responding to inbound sales inquiries (customer service)

- Processing orders (operations)

- Organizing/manipulating customer data (operations)

- Supervising staff (management)

- Meeting with leaders and colleagues inside the organization (management)

- Developing and implementing group marketing programs (management/marketing)

- Engaging in direct, outbound, persuasive communication with existing and potential clients, either on the phone or in person, preferably outside the office (sales)

How much of that pie is devoted to customer service and operations? Is this appropriate work for your senior sales staffer? Could someone else do this work more cost effectively?

How much of the pie is devoted to outbound, proactive sales activity?

Based on this breakdown of duties, is your senior sales staffer primarily a:

Manager?

Marketer?

Customer service representative?

Administrator?

Salesperson?

Do you have a senior sales staff person who isn't doing sales?

Can you restructure this position to allow for fifty percent of the time to be devoted to outbound sales activity and fifty percent to management and administration?

If you do, is your senior sales staffer prepared to do the work? Is he or she a *sales* person?

Is your group sales department a group order-taking department or has it earned its name?

Group Sales Is a Stand-Alone Function.

It happens all the time:

- Group sales offers a ten percent discount, but when single-ticket sales start to tank, marketing approves a single-ticket offer at twenty-five percent off. The offer is launched, and the groups who booked at ten percent go ballistic. After some unpleasant arguments everyone agrees that it was poor planning and that the group customers who complain loudly enough should get a rebate. Meanwhile, group customers vow, "Never again!"

- Or the full-page season ad breaks and there's no group phone number listed.

- Or management decides to front-load groups (force them to buy tickets early in the run) or limit their tickets to weekdays even if most of the B-to-B customers can't work that way.

- Or marketing decides to use the subscription brochure for groups—the one that says in huge block letters: SUBSCRIBERS GET THE BEST SEATS!

- Or the theatre launches a web site—the most powerful sales tool ever invented—and buries the group booking pages or neglects to include them.

- Or the box office gets busy with priority single-ticket offers and stops processing group confirmations for a week...or two weeks...or three week...or four weeks...

- Or the managing director storms into the group sales office in July shouting, "I don't care if it is summer, we're doing Shakespeare, so drop everything and get me student groups!"

- Or the GM says, "The show starts in one week and we've got empty seats out the wazoo—let's do some of that group sales stuff you proposed last year and see if we can't fill some previews."

- Or so many performances have been subscribed that the only group buyers who can book are low-end consumers and students who don't mind bad seats.

- Or the promotions director negotiates a deal that holds prime orchestra inventory for last-minute consumer business while there are stacks of full-price group requests that can't be confirmed.

- Or the senior group discount seats end up in the balcony—two flights up with no elevator.

- Or the house manager, who has decided that groups are a royal pain, rolls her eyes every time a bus pulls up and starts yelling and herding the group customers as if her day might have been perfect if this damned group hadn't just arrived.

- Or a discount email offer goes out to the employees of Acme Corporation after the group sales department convinced Acme's HR department to commit to ten groups of fifty tickets at full price.

- Or the show's producer decides groups make bad audiences and sales should be curtailed. Then sales start to tank and the policy is reversed, but only after all of the group buyers have been thoroughly offended.

- Or the box office allocates group inventory in lesser seating sections even though thirty percent of the buyers are corporate groups looking for prime, full-price locations.

- Or the whole-house buyout can't go through because the development department has a donor reception that night— or the artistic director thinks a seven-thirty start time is tacky —or the company manager doesn't want to bother pulling back house seat allocations—or the venue owner prohibits bundled singles (single-ticket sales bundled and processed together to qualify as a group)—or because nobody under-stands that buyouts are the single most efficient way to sell tickets!

- Or the producer of a national tour gets a request for twelve 700-seat theatre party bookings in major tour markets but can't sell the seats because no staffer in New York can take a few minutes to make the arrangements.

- Or the teachers can't book the fall show because the tickets didn't go on sale until summer recess.

- Or the designers of the new fifty million-dollar performing arts center forgot to think about bus access.

The list is very long, very real, and the blunders are repeated endlessly. Why? Because group sales is usually set aside as a stand-alone entity and is not integrated into the overall audience development strategy. There is very little communication between the group sales staff and the strategic decision makers, and there is virtually no communication between the people who buy the bulk inventory and entertainment industry leaders.

By shunting group sales off to the side and assuming it will function well enough on its own, we create a communication gap that severely diminishes the potential in volume sales. By endlessly repeating the same mistakes, we set up long-term animosities between the entertainment industry and the individuals who buy the most tickets. By institutionalizing some of these inconsistencies, we shut out lucrative new sources of incremental sales. High volume B-to-B buyers simply can't work with suppliers who don't take them into consideration in their strategic plans. They definitely won't work with suppliers who pull the rug out from under them at the last minute.

The fact that we have group sales customers at all is a striking indication that there is powerful demand in the marketplace. No matter how hard we beat these people up, they keep coming back for more. That is, *some* of them come back for more. Imagine what incremental sales we might generate if the customers we offended were motivated to stick around.

If we give group sales a place at the table, we'll make smart producing decisions using reliable information about group sales potential. We'll craft long-term strategic plans that anticipate group versus single-ticket conflicts. We'll make productive long-term pricing decisions that incentivize below-the-line advance wholesale purchases so we don't have to flood local single-ticket markets with last-minute discount offers. (Think about that one for a minute!) We'll develop productive sales partnerships with businesses that deliver customers to our doorstep. Most importantly, we'll avoid the tedious string of counterproductive errors that have been suppressing and disincentivizing group sales potential for years.

If we want group sales to be effective, we can't go on treating it like a bastard stepchild. Group sales should be a vital component of the stage entertainment industry's long-term audience development strategy and it must be treated as a legitimate member of the family.

Group Mythology Overview

The most cost-effective way to improve group sales is to reject the myths that have been suppressing potential for decades and replace them with new truths. Here's a quick review of the myths and the new truths that should become guiding principals instead.

MYTH: Groups are there to fill the seats you can't sell to the *real* customers.

NEW REALITY: Individuals who buy group tickets are real customers who deserve as much respect as single-ticket buyers because they are inexpensive to reach, because they buy so many tickets, and because they spend so much money on our products.

MYTH: Group sales is about selling tickets to consumers.

NEW REALITY: Increasingly group sales is about selling tickets to businesses but its potential is limited by an outdated consumer business model. We'll need to change our consumer-based methods if we want to maximize the potential for increased revenue in B-to-B markets.

MYTH: Bulk is beneath us.

NEW REALITY: Demonstrating respect and appreciation for customers who buy in bulk will increase yield from existing clients and encourage new customers.

MYTH:	Groups buy tickets.
NEW REALITY:	Group tickets are not purchased by groups; they're purchased by *individuals* who influence a lot of spending. These volume buyers are worth knowing, understanding, and speaking to with respect, gratitude, and magnanimity.
MYTH:	One size fits all.
NEW REALITY:	Customers come in different shapes and sizes so we need a sophisticated, dynamic, and flexible service model for maximizing their individual potential.
MYTH:	Group buyers are parasites.
NEW REALITY:	Group buyers are valuable selling partners who take our marketing messages to remote consumers, package our shows to make them more marketable, sell our tickets for us, and deliver customers to our doorstep.
MYTH:	They'll call back.
NEW REALITY:	Bad service is inexcusable. Giving good service is an inexpensive way to grow audiences and increase revenue.
MYTH:	Marketing to groups means modifying the consumer ads and brochures.
NEW REALITY:	Marketing to groups means knowing what motivates individual group buyers so we can antici-

pate their concerns, *persuade* them to order tickets, and give them the tools they need to sell tickets to others.

MYTH: The play's the thing.

NEW REALITY: For group buyers, the show is just a part of the package, and the package is often the make-or-break factor in a sale.

MYTH: Group sales is about sending flyers and answering calls.

NEW REALITY: Sales is about strategic, proactive, persuasive, person-to-person interaction with current and potential ticket buyers. Everything else is operations.

MYTH: Group sales is a stand-alone function.

NEW REALITY: Integrating group sales into the total audience development strategy will help us avoid costly mistakes, increase customer loyalty, and enable us to maximize potential from new sources.

The end result of rejecting the myths and embracing new group sales realities is more money in the coffers, more ticket holders in the seats, and healthier long-term audiences for American stage entertainment.

PART II

THE MARKETS

The following pages contain a breakdown of group sales markets.

Thinking about group sales in terms of different "buyer types" is relatively new to stage entertainment professionals but it is essential. Knowing our volume ticket markets enables us to understand what motivates buyers. Understanding these motivations enables us to speak to each market more persuasively and to serve each one more productively.

The markets outlined in this section cover most available buyers, but not all will be right for every show or venue. Ultimately, each group seller must decide which markets are right for his or her product(s). The important thing is to identify new markets that offer reasonable potential and then take bold, proactive steps toward developing them.

Meetings and Incentives

Category:	Business-to-Business

Sub-Markets:	Meeting and Convention Planners
	Destination Management Companies
	Special Event Planners
	Incentive Travel Professionals

The target markets in this category, sometimes referred to in industry jargon as "MICE" (meetings, incentives, conventions, and events), are at the corporate end of the group sales spectrum. Typically these buyers are business executives who work for large companies or they are executives at firms that subcontract with corporate clientele. Travel is central to their businesses because meetings and conventions take place in various destinations, and the most popular corporate incentives usually involve travel.

Meeting, incentive, and event professionals are an important target market for group sellers because they can deliver large groups, whole-house buyouts, and high-end, top-dollar business. Most cities with professional entertainment venues are also business hubs or popular travel destinations with busy convention centers, corporate hotels, and event venues; thus, the live entertainment/MICE connection is a natural.

MEETING AND CONVENTION PLANNERS

Meeting and convention planners coordinate gatherings for corporations, businesses, associations, special interest groups, etc. They plan meetings of all sizes, from small local get-togethers to large "citywide" conventions with many thousands of delegates. Planners select cities, secure venues, set schedules, coordinate local transportation, and arrange travel and accommodations, among other duties. Meeting planners are also called upon to provide entertainment or leisure activities for meeting participants, convention delegates and/or their spouses. Some meeting planners are independent and some work in-house for the corporations and associations they serve.

DESTINATION MANAGEMENT COMPANIES (DMCs)

DMCs provide local meeting and event services for remote clients. For example, if Acme National Products is based in Boston but is having a regional sales meeting in Denver, the company might prefer to hire a Denver-based DMC to put together the meeting for them. Unlike meeting planners, DMCs serve clients who may be looking for leisure activities as well as meeting services. They may offer their services to incentive travel companies, tour operators, and/or meeting planners.

DMCs are local experts and are therefore prepared to offer out-of-town clients a complete range of goods and services to support their gathering, group visit, or event. Entertainment always figures prominently in their planning and an existing show can be easier for a DMC to use than an event that has to be booked or produced for the occasion.

EVENT PLANNERS

Event planners plan parties, events, and celebrations of all kinds. They provide this service to a wide variety of clients including meeting planners, DMCs, corporations, charities, associations, and organizations of every conceivable description. Event planners work with local clients as well as with visiting business groups. They are always on the lookout for exciting, original entertainment ideas so pre- or post-show parties can be extremely attractive possibilities.

INCENTIVE COMPANIES

Incentive companies and in-house incentive executives create travel packages—often group packages—to motivate and reward corporate employees. These packages usually involve luxury travel with high-end accommodations and VIP entertainment products. For example, if Acme National Products hires Baker & Baker Corporate Incentives to send their top salespeople to Las Vegas, group sellers in Vegas need to be on Baker & Baker's radar.

Companies that deal with meetings, conventions, incentives, and corporate events handle groups of all sizes, and the larger ones can handle whole house buyouts with relative ease. Because they are dealing with corporate budgets, they are often prepared to spend on quality top dollar entertainment products. Because they are extremely busy, however, they tend to look for turnkey programs that don't require excessive work.

Meeting, incentive, and event professionals work with businesses and corporate clients worldwide so they reach into diverse, far-flung markets made up of all types of consumers who are often traveling and looking for leisure activities. Working with these buyers enables local stage entertainment providers to dramatically expand their sales and marketing reach.

WHAT MICE WANT FROM YOU

- Service appropriate for high-level corporate executives who direct the expenditure of millions of dollars in cities through out North America

- Advance schedule information and access to available show dates before smaller local consumer groups

- Flexible, long-lead booking with custom payment terms that reflect and/or reward volume ticket purchases

- Customized ticketing services for bundled singles, if available

- Information and contacts for goods and services that support or augment the entertainment event such as party venues, transportation, catering, etc.

- VIP packages and value-added extras for high-end incentives

- Creative ideas from the venue for packaging the show

HOW TO CATCH MICE

Most cities have a convention and visitors bureau (CVB) that strives to bring meetings, conventions, and incentives into their communities. These CVBs should be able to provide a list of organizations that have planned or are planning a meeting in the community. They are usually able to supply their members with the name of the company that's planning the meeting and the name of the meeting planner. They will also know and work with all local destination management companies and event companies. If you don't already belong, join your CVB and get to know the staff members who market and sell your community as a corporate business destination. They can provide a wealth of useful information. Local hotels also host meetings, conventions, and incentive groups so their sales executives will be good contacts to make and nurture, too.

Your local chapter of Meeting Professionals International (MPI) can be a great resource for networking. If the meetings market is right for your product, join MPI, get to know the local members, and use the association's marketing tools to reach out to inbound corporate groups from all over the world. Try Society of Incentive Travel Executives (SITE) for the incentive side.

Get to know all the DMCs and event planners in your community; find out what they do and how your product can be used to enhance the gatherings they plan for their clients.

TIPS FOR SUCCESS WITH MICE

Be professional. These are business executives who spend millions of dollars and are accustomed to working with other professionals of their caliber. Do your homework. Know exactly what you are selling and how it will satisfy your clients' needs. Don't waste their time. Stay focused on how booking your show will make their job easier or more profitable.

Be realistic. These buyers will be most interested in popular entertainment familiar to their clients. They may respond to less popular shows that have a strong connection to the group they're serving (you might sell a classical music event to a music educators convention, for example), but you'll need to be more persuasive. In general, corporate executives are unlikely to take risks on unknown products.

Be willing to offer familiarization visits to prospective customers (FAM tours), and make sure your CVB, your DMCs, and your local hotel sales executives know they can bring hot prospects in to see your shows. If you can spare the tickets, there's no better way to land a corporate group than to give the meeting planner a preview of what he/she is buying. If they're an extremely hot prospect and you don't have spare tickets, buy them house seats out of your own budget!

Establish strong relationships in your community with all the local DMCs and event planners. Make a point of learning about their businesses and make sure they know about yours. If you have opportunities to invite guests to your shows, put your area DMCs on the top of your invite list.

Get to know all the other local businesses that market themselves to meeting professionals, event planners, and DMCs. Partner with these businesses when appropriate and maintain high visibility in the conventions, meetings, events, and travel and hospitality business communities.

Finally, if your facility is available as a corporate meeting or party venue, or if you are in an unusually glamorous location, don't forget that MICE are always on the lookout for interesting venues. Teaming up with your facility's catering sales staff or building rental managers can be a win-win proposition.

Bundled Singles and/or Super Groups:

Distributing tickets to large groups is a complex, time-consuming job that few professional group buyers want to do. Having to collect money and hand out tickets often prevents corporate buyers from embracing whole-house buyouts or large theatre parties.

You may be able to eliminate this obstacle for them by collecting payments from and distributing tickets to individual members of their group. The buyers will deliver the group sales and promote the purchase of tickets but you will be responsible for doing the administrative work. This process is referred to as *bundled singles* or *super groups* and it is a useful way to serve untapped B-to-B markets.

I once sold two performances of a long-running show to a meeting planner who was organizing a convention in San Francisco. She wanted her delegates to be able to see the show but didn't want to have to sell the tickets. So we worked together to solve her problem in a way that benefited everyone involved. Here is the basic structure of the deal we came up with:

- We reserved two performances at the approved group price of ten percent off.

- We asked the meeting planner to advertise the show to her delegates and give them our contact information for orders.

- The majority of Orchestra and Mezzanine seats were priced at seventy-five dollars so the group rate we charged for these seats was sixty-seven fifty.

- We added a five dollar service fee to cover our processing costs and to cover a one dollar per ticket incentive for the meeting planner, so delegates were paying seventy-two fifty, a price lower than the original face value.

- One of the performances was a Saturday night so the theatre didn't pay a commission, but the commission from the other full house and the small income from the per-ticket fee made the deal worthwhile.

It was a win-win-win deal all around. The producer of the show sold two houses that wouldn't have sold otherwise. We as the group agent earned a buyout commission on one house plus a small fee on each of the 3,600 tickets. The convention delegates got great entertainment at an exclusive price, and the meeting planner got to offer excellent service while earning income for her efforts.

Some ticketing businesses may argue that bundling interferes with their contractual right to distribute individual ticket inventory, but most group agreements don't define the process sufficiently to preclude bundling. Since most bundled singles programs tap new markets that can't be tapped in any other way, obstructing the bundled singles process can be counterproductive.

If your organization can service the individual orders by phone, fax, or email, try offering bundled group services to bring in more buyouts and high-end corporate group business. If you can't service the orders, consider subcontracting a phone room and paying out a portion of the fee to cover processing.

Domestic Group Tour Operators

Category:	Business-to-Business
Sub-Markets:	Domestic Long-Haul Tour Operators
	Regional Day-Trip Tour Operators
	Student and Youth Tour Operators

LONG-HAUL GROUP TOUR OPERATORS

North American long-haul group tour operators create travel packages for traveling groups (preformed groups) and for unrelated individuals who may travel together in groups as a result of having purchased packages (retail tours). These tours serve every conceivable destination in the U.S. and Canada, including most live entertainment markets. Tours can range from short jaunts to multi-week excursions. Entertainment ranks among the top three activities on group tours so stage entertainment is always a popular product.

The primary market for long-haul tour operators is seniors, although many companies are working hard to tap aging baby boomer markets with tours that offer more stimulation and more opportunities for independent activity.

Since most live entertainment markets are also popular visitor destinations, group sellers may discover that North American tour operators are already visiting their cities. The trick is to find out which operators are already visiting and which entertainment activities they are booking during their stays. The local convention and visitors bureau (CVB) should be able to help you with this information.

Long-haul tour operators are interested in popular entertainment products that are reasonably consistent so they can book marketable entertainment throughout the year. Producers and presenters of diverse products or short-running shows will have a harder time getting long-haul tour operators' attention. The most important thing is to make sure that the operators who are sending tours to the area have performance schedules well in advance. They won't necessarily find every show appropriate, but at least they'll have the information they need when the show does fit the group.

There are several ways to research long-haul operators. The best place to start is with your local destination marketing organization, which is usually the CVB. A good CVB will track visiting groups closely and be able to provide solid data on the operators to target. You may also want to identify the hotels that serve these visiting tour groups and speak with their group sales executives. These folks will have excellent relationships with the tour operator clients they serve. Other group attractions and service providers will have detailed information about visiting group tour operators, but the more competitive ones may not want to share their information.

There are several trade associations that serve domestic tour operators and their suppliers. The larger associations include the United States Tour Operators Association (USTOA), the National Tour Association (NTA), and the American Bus Association (ABA). There are regional associations such as Travel South and Ontario Motor Coach Association; ownership groups such as TAP (a collective of NTA operators); International Motor Coach Group; and various state or local government organizations that support, regulate, or market to the group tour industry. Your CVB will probably belong to the important associations and can help you gain access, provided you are a member of the bureau.

DAY-TRIP TOUR OPERATORS

Day-trip tour operators create travel packages that span one or two days so they tend to involve destinations within a set region. They like stage entertainment because a show with a meal and transportation makes a perfect day-trip itinerary.

Day-trip tour operators are among a venue's or show's most important customers. They enhance a show's marketability by including it in a package; they enhance a show's marketing reach by advertising their packages to proprietary group markets (markets to which only they have access); and they are usually steady customers who can be counted on year after year. In many markets the larger day-trip tour operators qualify as top customers because they buy more tickets and spend more money than other ticket buyers. (In terms of dollars and ticket sales, they are far ahead of charter subscribers and the most avid single-ticket buyers.)

Day-trip operators capture group business from long-established group clientele or from local consumers who prefer the convenience of buying a package rather than booking the show themselves. Most group ticket sellers will already have local day-trip operators on their lists, but this doesn't mean they've tapped their day-trip markets effectively. Many day-trip operators complain that local shows and venues don't give them the service they need to maximize their show package business.

The most important day-trip tour operators are the companies located in population centers just outside the venue's media market as they deliver consumers who aren't necessarily reached by local advertising, such as Sacramento/San Francisco, Milwaukee/Chicago, Hartford/Boston, and Birmingham/Atlanta. These operators can become vital marketing partners who have a vested interest in delivering customers to a given show.

Most group ticket sellers already derive huge benefits from regional day-trip operators without actually courting them. Those who actually reach out to day-trip operators, however, will discover significant untapped potential. Those who recognize and reward high-volume operators will find loyal, long-term partners, who become indispensable extensions of their sales and marketing efforts.

Most venues will find day-trip operators on their existing group sales database. Otherwise, a simple online search under local "bus tours" or "sightseeing tours" should call up lists of most of the day-trip operators in any area.

STUDENT AND YOUTH TOUR OPERATORS

Student and youth tour operators provide travel services to school groups and youth organizations such as bands, choirs, theatre groups, and other extracurricular organizations. These traveling students come from everywhere and travel to destinations throughout North America. Popular destinations include areas that are rich in historical or educational significance and ones that offer performance opportunities for music and theatre groups.

Student and youth tour operators will be interested in popular shows, but they may be interested in a broad range of theatre and performing arts offerings as well. The tours usually have an educational thrust, so operators want quality entertainment that satisfies educational requirements or lets parents and teachers know there is credible content. Shows with educational support materials, such as study guides and videos, will have a leg up.

Since many of the tours are designed to provide performance opportunities for traveling bands and choirs, operators will ask if there are performance opportunities at the venue. Creative group sellers may want to arrange for visiting performing groups to entertain audiences in public areas outside the venue. This can be a win-win approach to satisfying the operators' needs while selling student group ticket inventory. Students can offer a forty-five-minute preshow concert for arriving guests and stow their gear in the coaches before taking their seats inside. The venue gets the sale and the kids get to perform at the venue. Win-win.

As with long-haul tour operators, the best place to find information about student/youth operators is your CVB, the salespeople at the hotels they use, and other group attractions and service providers in your area. Otherwise, look into the Student Youth Travel Association (SYTA), the National Tour Association (NTA), or the American Bus Association (ABA).

74

WHAT DOMESTIC TOUR OPERATORS NEED

- Advance information on show schedules with complete date ranges (even if they are not advertised to local consumers)

- Service appropriate for business people in a customer service industry who must pass on excellent service to their clientele

- Information about other group opportunities and attractions in the venue's community

- Information about the show so they can communicate effectively with their people

- Marketing and educational materials so they can "sell" the show to their clients or highlight its educational value

- An ongoing relationship with the group seller so that they are always up on long-lead opportunities

- Flexible booking with custom payment terms that diminish risk for the operator without undue risk to the venue or show

- Pricing incentives that reflect and reward volume business

TIPS FOR SUCCESS WITH TOUR OPERATORS

Do your homework. Know which operators visit your area and target the ones with the most potential.

Understand that your show is only a part of the tour experience. Be prepared to describe how your product augments their itineraries and how it benefits their customers. It also helps to be able to describe how it will help the operator make more money. And the easier you can make it for the operators, the better your chances of getting their business.

Know the logistics of group travel. You have to understand the timing, the travel intervals between attractions, and all the access and parking issues. You may have the best possible product, but if it doesn't fit into an itinerary, you can't make the sale.

Get the information out early! Some operators need twelve to eighteen months of lead time.

Take time to learn how the operators do business. When you sell to them, you become a travel industry supplier, which means you are in the travel business. If you're in the business, you need to understand how it works.

Make your local day-trip tour operators your best friends. Arrange for the top performers to have lunch with your CEO, executive director or top administrator. No good executive leader will refuse to have lunch with his or her biggest customers. At lunch, ask them questions about their success with your product, then ask them what you can do to help them sell more entertainment packages. Listen to what they tell you and work hard to meet their needs.

Put your local tour operator contacts at the top of your VIP list and don't forget their staff. Reward them for their patronage with appropriate VIP service: advance insider information, discounts, commissions (yes, commissions), free tickets, reception invitations. Do anything you can to help them buy and sell more of your product.

Join appropriate group travel industry trade associations, be an active participant and understand that sales is about relationships as much as it is about the desirability of the product or the quality of your sales pitch. Go to every social event, meet as many people as you can—and have a good time with them.

Corporations and Businesses

Category:	Business-to-Business
Market:	Local corporations and businesses

This is a huge category containing businesses of all sizes that are engaged in every conceivable trade. The reason we target businesses is that they tend to contain populations of like-minded potential ticket buyers who can be reached through their companies. We also target businesses because they often have individuals or departments that are motivated to organize group events and/or buy group tickets.

It is perhaps useful to differentiate local businesses from the preceding meeting, event and incentive markets. Here, "corporations and businesses" refer to companies that function in the region where the venue or show is located.

In general, businesses buy tickets to entertain clients or to motivate employees. Client entertainment can be things such as hosting a group of foreign business executives, luring potential buyers with the promise of a show, organizing elaborate sales events, or simply keeping a pile of tickets on hand for incidental client gifts.

Motivating employees can take the form of structured incentive and activity programs at large corporations or less formal employee rewards such as holiday gatherings or casual employee outings organized by those who have a specific interest in stage entertainment.

Corporations that are willing to use email or pay envelope stuffers to disseminate ticket information can be extraordinary resources for bundled singles programs. These are organizations that like to use their internal communications networks to pass on exclusive perks to their employees. Group sellers can use companies like these to extend group discounts to select populations and assemble the groups internally.

A challenge for group sellers with corporations and businesses is to find the decision makers in the company. Businesses buy tickets for so many reasons that there is little consistency from one business to the next, so finding the group ticket buyers in local companies can be a long, frustrating process. Sometimes the process is more costly than the return on the investment. Add to this the fact that your marketing department may be offering tickets in trade, or they may be offering exclusive corporate single-ticket discounts, or your development department may be asking for contributed income, and the picture gets complicated quickly.

Group ticket sellers who tap and serve corporate markets successfully, however, will find productive long-term clients who deliver dependable high-end business. Those that develop strong relationships with employee services and recreation staff, HR staff, and/or PR departments will find excellent group potential and interesting opportunities for bundled singles and below-the-line discount offers.

WHAT LOCAL BUSINESSES NEED

- Service appropriate for business people at all levels from CEOs to informal employee group organizers

- Access to additional facilities for dining and/or receptions at or near the venue

- Information about the show so they can communicate effectively with their people

- Marketing materials

- An ongoing relationship with the group seller so that they are always up on long-lead opportunities

- Flexible booking with custom payment terms that reflect and/or reward the size of the purchase

- Collaborative bundled singles programs that are integrated through all venue departments including marketing, development, and management

HOW TO REACH LOCAL BUSINESSES

To locate local businesses, start by searching your database and identifying all the corporate buyers on the list. Conduct a mini research campaign by contacting those people and asking them how and why they buy tickets from you. Apply what you learn to other potential buyers in the business community.

Seek out non-competitive partners who serve the same markets (restaurants, event venues, caterers) and negotiate cooperative promotions. There is no better way to reach out to corporate buyers than through a partner's pre-existing database of local business clients. Or, find the group sales directors from the largest football, basketball, or baseball teams in town. Take them out to lunch to learn what they know about corporate sales. They tend to be tied into the business community and may be willing to share advice. You may even want to hire an outbound telemarketer with past sports sales experience.

If your organization is not-for-profit, think about using existing fundraising relationships with local businesses to find useful group sales contacts. Board members should be able to provide inside access to the local business community as well. It is easier to sell to local businesses if they have a pre-existing relationship with the venue, especially if there is an advocate working on the inside.

Another good method for reaching corporate buyers is through commercially available mailing lists from companies that specialize in corporate gifts, such as specialty foods, gift baskets, fruits, candies, wines, or motivational merchandise. These contacts are more likely to be the individuals who influence client entertainment or incentive purchase decisions.

Go where the ticket brokers go. If you see ads for ticket brokers in your local business publications, think about placing a group sales ad there too.

Join and participate in as many business groups as possible in order to make quality contacts. Start with your chamber of commerce and expand from there.

TIPS FOR SUCCESS WITH BUSINESSES

Use available lists of corporate buyers carefully remembering that mining for group decision makers is tough work even for the most talented cold callers.

Read your local business publications and get in the habit of culling leads from among the people mentioned. Prepare a model letter and send one or two personalized versions every week to likely sources.

Be active and visible in your business communities so people know whom to call when they want to book a group. Be sharply focused, however, and make certain you are networking with the right people; find the group buyers whenever possible and court them assertively.

Maintain strong relationships with the people who do buy so you will earn their long-term business. As the cliché goes, it is ten times more expensive to get a new customer than to keep an old one.

Use the resources that are already available to you. If your organization has board members from the business community, work with your development department to find out how they can help. If your marketing department is developing cooperative marketing programs with local businesses, suggest that they make an employee night part of the deal and offer to bundle those single-ticket sales into a group event. Otherwise, go to the businesses from which your organization buys goods and services and leverage that relationship into a group sales relationship.

Be flexible, be creative, and above all, be professional. Business people want to do business with other business people, and your jeans and T-shirt organizational culture may not fly with them.

International Travel Markets

Category:	Business-to-Business
Sub-Markets:	International Tour Operators and Wholesalers Receptive Tour Operators

International travel markets are not for everyone. Typically, the group sellers who will benefit from working with international tour operators are:

- Venues and shows in major international destination cities: New York, Las Vegas, Los Angeles, San Francisco and Orlando, for example

- Shows that appeal to non-English speaking visitors

- Venues and/or shows that are internationally branded: Radio City Music Hall, *The Lion King*, the Hollywood Bowl, Cirque du Soleil, for example

- Venues with consistent offerings that can be advertised many months in advance

INTERNATIONAL WHOLESALERS AND TOUR OPERATORS

International wholesalers and tour operators sell packaged vacations and business travel services to traveling consumers and groups. They operate in nearly every country throughout the world and deliver millions of travelers into North America every year. The group portion of their business is small relative to their individual business, and it is diminishing as foreigners become more comfortable traveling independently in the U.S. and Canada.

RECEPTIVE TOUR OPERATORS

Receptive tour operators work locally to package North American destinations for remote tour operators. So if a group tour operator wants to send a group to Chicago, but knows nothing about the destination, he/she may rely on the receptive operator to pull together the package components. Receptives are important middlemen in a chain that helps remote tour operators gain access to goods and services in a given destination without having to be experts or have sales contacts in that particular area.

A receptive will contract with suppliers of travel package components (airfare, hotel, ground transportation, sightseeing, transfers, entertainment tickets, theme park admissions, for example) and sell these products to remote tour operators working in foreign countries. These packages are typically sold in travel agencies. Groups may buy packages or they may have their tour customized to meet their needs.

The most important thing to remember in dealing with international tour operators and receptives is that they are middlemen and expect to make money. The prices you charge and the incentives you offer to middlemen will determine how useful these customers will be in buying and reselling tickets to your show(s).

International operators who buy stage entertainment tickets in advance are usually doing so for Broadway shows and perhaps for shows in Las Vegas. For the most part, international wholesalers and receptive tour operators are not accessing stage entertainment in other markets because the product is too variable to promote in advance or the venues are unaccustomed or unwilling to work with international buyers.

WHAT INTERNATIONAL TRAVEL BUYERS NEED

- Advance information on show schedules with complete date ranges (even if they are not advertised to local consumers)

- Service appropriate for business people who must extend excellent service to their clientele and who serve people from different cultures

- Information about other group services and attractions in the venue's community

- Information about the show so they can communicate effectively with their clients

- Marketing materials

- An ongoing relationship with the venue so that they are always aware of long-lead opportunities

- Flexible booking with custom payment terms that diminish risk for the operator without undue risk to the show or venue

HOW TO REACH INTERNATIONAL TOUR OPERATORS

Go to your convention and visitors bureau and ask for advice on targeting international markets. If the experts at the bureau think international markets are a good match for your product, ask for their assistance in getting started. A good CVB should have complete details about which countries are sending travelers into their market and which wholesalers and receptives are generating the most business. It is in the CVB's interest to help local attractions market themselves effectively to international buyers. They won't do the marketing for you, but they should be able to provide the information and opportunities necessary for you to get the job done.

Seek out other businesses that target international group business. Take time to learn what they do and ask for their candid advice about whether or not it is right for you. Partner, when appropriate, with other products in your community, such as hotels, restaurants, ground transportation providers, and non-competitive attractions.

Join the Travel Industry Association of America (TIA) and access their exhaustive library of information on the international travel industry. Consider attending TIA's annual Pow-Wow, a marketplace designed to showcase North American destinations and travel products to the international travel industry. Otherwise, join Receptive Services Association of America (RSAA), learn more about receptive tour operators, and take advantage of marketing opportunities aimed at the receptive industry.

TIPS FOR SUCCESS WITH INTERNATIONALS

It takes at least three years to tap into international group markets so you'll want to start with a three-year plan. Know exactly what countries and companies you are going to target, how you are going to target them, and what kind of return you expect to see on your investment. Start small, get some successes under your belt, then branch out.

Team up with others in your market. The best results come when your destination markets itself as a whole. Marketing internationally can also be expensive so cooperative marketing can be considerably more cost effective.

Be smart. Listen and learn. Don't try to sell a product that a group from Milan, Osaka, or Buenos Aires wouldn't thoroughly enjoy.

Understand that you are working with different people from different cultures who speak different languages. Be sensitive to those differences and defer to them whenever possible.

Remember that when you are speaking to an international buyer, that person is someone who must filter your message for his or her customers. Make it simple and direct. Provide pre-designed images whenever possible. Double-check the translation of your message to avoid embarrassing mistakes.

Be especially sensitive to issues of timing as international travel companies need long lead times to market your product. Some will begin advertising their travel packages twelve to eighteen months in advance.

Be flexible and willing to innovate. International wholesalers and receptives may ask for services that differ from those normally offered. If they want six tickets per show for every show at the group rate, think about the value of extending group benefits across multiple performances.

A Word About FITs:

Good group ticket sellers inevitably come into contact with B-to-B customers who want to know if they can access tickets on an FIT basis. Here's a little primer on FITs:

FIT is a travel industry term that distinguishes individual travelers from groups. In our industry we say *groups* or *single tickets*, in the tourism industry they say *groups* or *FITs*. It's that easy.

But there is one more distinguishing factor. FIT is a B-to-B term that refers to travelers who buy travel packages as individuals rather than as members of a group. Anyone can walk into a travel agency or go online and buy a vacation package—five days in Las Vegas including airfare, hotel, a trip to the Grand Canyon, and tickets to *Blue Man Group*—without having to go with twenty other people. That's because vacation packages are sold to individuals on an FIT basis.

Travel packages or vacation packages are put together by wholesale vacation packagers who arrange with airlines, hotels, and attractions to buy their products on an FIT basis a few at a time rather than in large blocks.

These wholesale vacation packagers are middlemen who make their money buying and reselling travel products. The products they buy for resale to individuals are known as FITs because they are purchased for, and resold to, foreign independent travelers.

The likeliest root for the acronym FIT is foreign independent traveler, but some say it is frequent independent traveler, or foreign individual traveler. The origins don't really matter. What's important is that the expression FIT has come to refer to the individual products that are purchased by packagers for resale to individual travelers.

Here's a specific example. A couple in Berlin walks into a travel agency to make plans for a ten-day trip to the American

West. They especially want to see Las Vegas, and they want to see a hit show while they're there. The travel agent goes to the rack and pulls out a brochure—provided to her by a wholesale vacation packager—containing travel package options for individual travelers. The travel agent helps the couple pick the package they want, including a three-day stay in Vegas with tickets to a major show, and she books the package for them by contacting the packager that produced the brochure. Soon afterward, the couple gets a packet containing the itinerary with all the necessary tickets and vouchers.

HOW DO FIT VACATION PACKAGERS MAKE MONEY?

A fair amount of work went in to assembling all the package components and promoting the package so the whole-sale vacation packager wants to earn something for his efforts. And the travel agent did a good job of selling the package to the consumers so she deserves a reasonable commission. To make sure everyone gets compensated fairly, the hotels, transportation providers, attractions, shows, and sightseeing tours agree to offer "insider" or "wholesale" or "net" rates that are lower than the published consumer prices.

Naturally, the couple in Berlin wants to pay a reasonable price so their tickets will have to be priced in such a way that the wholesale vacation packager and travel agent can earn mark-ups without having to overcharge the consumers. Here's a simplified version of how that might work if the ticket normally sells for a box office price of one hundred dollars:

The box office agrees to sell the one hundred dollar ticket to the wholesale vacation packager for eighty, thus netting eighty on the sale.

The wholesale vacation packager includes the ticket in the package at a consumer price of one hundred dollars so the couple in Berlin can pay the same price they would pay at the box office. This leaves the wholesale vacation packager a potential earnings margin of twenty dollars.

The wholesale vacation packager must pay a commission to the travel agent, however. If he has agreed to pay the travel agent ten percent, she gets ten dollars, leaving him ten dollars.

It is a win-win-win-win situation. The show wins because it sells two tickets it would not otherwise have sold. The wholesale vacation packager wins because he gets to sell a quality package featuring reasonably priced entertainment—and earn ten percent. The agent wins because she gets to sell a quality package featuring reasonably priced entertainment—and earn ten percent. The folks in Berlin win because they get to buy a quality package and won't have to worry about getting tickets when they arrive.

WHY WOULD WE WANT TO SELL FITs IF WE'RE NETTING ONLY EIGHTY PERCENT?

- Packagers buy in bulk so they deserve rewards for their volume purchases

- Packagers market our products in places our marketing messages can't reach

- Selling tickets in advance is a more dependable way to make sure visitors get tickets to our shows

- Packagers provide a dependable, long-term source of advance purchases that can lessen our dependence on local consumers

- Discounting to remote packagers preserves full-price integrity in our local markets

- Entertainment is one of the top three activities sought by travelers

- Asking customers to pay for tickets in advance as a part of the package price can make the expense more palatable than expecting them to make last minute cash purchase decisions

- Travelers trust their travel agents more than they do the various ticket resellers they encounter when they travel. Who wouldn't?

- Packagers deliver ticketholders to our doors

- We can offer below-the-line specials to wholesalers to stimulate greater seasonal sales without having to taint the local market with discount offers

WHAT DO FITs HAVE TO DO WITH GROUP SALES?

FITs are bulk purchases so they often fall into the groups category. Group sellers are also the travel industry's primary point of contact with the entertainment industry, so FIT buyers find themselves banging on the group door. Our challenge is to find ways to accommodate volume FIT buyers who want access to group discounts and incentives, even though their way of doing business doesn't fit into the old B-to-C group sales mold.

Ultimately, the issue boils down to volume sales versus one-off (here today, gone tomorrow) consumer sales. Group sales is the volume sales end of our business. The question is, can our volume sales policies—fifteen or more for one show—be expanded to accommodate volume ticket sales of fewer than fifteen per show across multiple performances?

Strategic Selling Partners

Category:	Business-to-Business
Sub-Markets:	Local Group Attractions
	Local Group Service Providers
	Destination Marketing
	Organizations

Strategic partners are non-competitive local group attractions, service providers, and destination marketing organizations that have an interest in developing cooperative sales initiatives. There is no better way to expand the market for groups than to team up with other group sales organizations that have compatible goals. Forming strategic relationships with these partners will:

- Add market appeal to your show by making it part of a package

- Add value to your show by pricing the package below what the components would cost individually

- Make purchasing your show more user friendly by offering one-stop package shopping

- Add market reach to your message by expanding available resources such as group sales databases, direct sales representation, direct marketing and media

- Offer expertise from seasoned sales professionals in more commercial sales environments

- Provide opportunities for tapping and developing new group sales markets

LOCAL GROUP ATTRACTIONS

Local group attractions include theme parks, shopping complexes, cultural and historic sites, museums, zoos, parks, sightseeing companies, and entertainment providers of all kinds. Many attractions aggressively market to groups and most welcome non-competitive cooperative opportunities to increase their group business through win-win joint promotions.

LOCAL GROUP SERVICE PROVIDERS

Service providers include businesses such as hotels, restaurants, event venues, ground transportation companies, and tour guides. Most of these companies court group business in an assertive manner, and most will welcome package opportunities that add value or appeal to their services.

DESTINATION MARKETING ORGANIZATIONS

Destination marketing organizations (DMOs) facilitate the marketing of a given destination to likely visitors. These include convention and visitors bureaus, government tourism agencies, chambers of commerce, local tourism-related trade associations, tourism marketing collectives, and strategic alliances among independent marketers. These organizations offer opportunities to market your product jointly and more efficiently with other attractions and services in your community.

Strategic partners understand that groups need one-stop shopping for dining, lodging, entertainment, and other leisure, cultural, or educational activities. The benefits of cooperative sales and marketing apply to them as well, so smart partners will be open to opportunities that are mutually beneficial.

Group business is extremely important to hotels. If there are hotels in your community, you can be certain they have full-time sales executives working to book groups of every kind. Some larger hotels will have multiple group sales executives, each dedicated to a different group market. Every group that visits your community for more than a day will be staying in some form of commercial lodging, and many will be looking for quality evening entertainment. What better way to reach visiting groups than through the hotel sales executives?

Group business is also vital to charter bus companies. Most good charter companies will have extraordinary regional group mailing lists, so partnering with them can open up vast new resources. Many charter companies provide local services to visiting groups so they have access to both local and remote group buyers.

Strategic partners won't necessarily buy tickets from you, although some may. They are more likely to refer clients to you or work with you on promoting packages that include your product.

Successful destination packages will include compatible products that satisfy the needs of group buyers in the simplest, most attractive, and most cost-efficient manner. A good show packaged with a local restaurant and a nearby shopping complex can make a perfect day-trip itinerary. (Those who turn up their noses at the mention of shopping should know that shopping tops the list of things people say they want to do when they travel. And that's not just limited to groups.)

Your local strategic partners will reach out to different markets or to groups with slightly different interests. This cross-fertilization of sales and marketing efforts offers excellent opportunities to carry your message to new customers who might not have considered stage entertainment when planning their visits. It also opens the door to new group sales databases that contain names yours may be missing.

Ultimately, strategic partnerships will consist of quality personal and professional relationships between your group sales operation and the sales executives who represent the other quality group products and services in your community.

WHAT THEY NEED

- Advance information on show schedules with complete date ranges (even if they are not advertised to local single-ticket buyers)

- Service commensurate with the level of service offered by the partners to their clients

- Information about the show so they can communicate effectively with their clientele

- Marketing materials

- An ongoing relationship with the group seller that includes periodic personal interaction with sales executives

- Direct access to the group booking infrastructure for details on availability and for tracking orders

- Complimentary ticket incentives for their bookings and/or FAM tickets for prospective clients

HOW TO REACH LOCAL PARTNERS

Go to your CVB membership directory and pick out all the hotels and other member companies that offer group products and services. Make a list of the companies that offer a product that could be packaged with your show or venue. Begin the process by meeting with the primary group sales person from each of these companies.

Find out as much as you can about how these group sales professionals do their jobs. If they belong to professional organizations that facilitate sales, consider joining the same organizations. Make use of your memberships and take advantage of all networking opportunities. Listen to your colleagues and learn from them.

Contact your local charter bus companies and offer to cover the cost of doing a joint mailing to their group lists. Work with them on a pitch that includes seeing your show and chartering one of their coaches. Who can refuse a win-win promotion when you are footing the bill?

Share information and resources whenever appropriate. Consider trading your database with non-competitive partners; cooperative exchanges are far more valuable in the long run than overzealous guarding of proprietary lists. Propose package promotions and then cross-sell those packages with your partners for expanded reach. Join together with multiple group sales partners to promote your venue neighborhood as a group destination for local, regional and remote visitors.

TIPS FOR SUCCESS WITH PARTNERS

Give as much as you request. Make your database available to non-competitive partners when they offer theirs to you. Make referrals to your partners' businesses as often as possible and include them whenever you can in your web listings or brochures.

Give more than you request. If your venue ever needs to fill empty seats on press nights or openings, consider extending offers to your sales partners and their co-workers. Papering with people who influence sales is a lot better than papering with seat fillers who have no outside influence.

Be personable and friendly. The better your relationships with your partners, the more productive your cross-selling partnerships will be.

Be a supportive destination marketing partner. Professionals who focus on making the pie bigger will always prevail over people who quibble over the size of their slice.

Affinity Organizations

Category:	Business-to-Business
Markets:	Membership Organizations

Affinity organizations are membership groups that benefit from solidifying their relationships with their constituents. The list of such organizations is long and it includes a wide array of different types of groups.

Stage entertainment can play a role in adding value to the affinity relationship by offering exclusive access to a show, by serving as the focus of an event, by providing the entertainment for a separate gathering, or by serving as the primary draw for gatherings with other agendas. Events that can be planned in conjunction with a show include fund-raisers, membership development events, events that add value to membership, events that reinforce affinity with the organization, or gatherings that simply make membership in a particular group more meaningful. A short list of affinity group types worth targeting might include:

- Local charities and local chapters of national and international charities

- Alumni organizations, fraternities, and sororities

- Trade associations, professional societies, guilds, unions, leagues, and academies

- Special interest organizations that have a unique affinity with the show you are selling

- Political or cause-related organizations

- Ethnic community organizations

- Leisure activity and leisure interest, avocation or hobby-related collectives

Affinity organizations can plan events of all sizes from intimate gatherings of VIPs to whole-house buyouts. Affinity organizations are especially interesting if you are selling a show that has specific subject matter. No matter how unusual or obscure the subject of the show you are selling, there is likely an organization whose members have an interest in that subject.

There is no limit to the potential offered by affinity organizations but it takes time and creativity to reach out to them. In the end, all it takes is one good contact, however, to come up with a major theatre party, a whole-house buyout, a pre-sale of a large block of tickets, or a loyal buyer of multiple groups in every season.

Producers of touring productions should note that national membership organizations can offer extraordinary opportunities for selling millions of dollars worth of tickets in cities across the country. The right match between show and charity could result in pre-sold whole-house buyouts in every tour city! A little advance planning and some centralized sales efforts could do in one meeting what dozens of group sales departments take months to accomplish on a market-by-market basis.

WHAT AFFINITY ORGANIZATIONS NEED

- Service appropriate for business executives who manage large membership organizations

- Access to or advice on additional facilities for dining and/or receptions at or near the venue

- Information about the show they can use to communicate effectively with their membership populations

- Support in the form of marketing materials or possibly even shared costs of mailings

- An ongoing relationship with the group seller or producer on a local or national level so that they are always up on long-lead opportunities

- Centralized booking mechanisms for national tours

- Flexible booking with custom payment terms that reflect and/or reward the size of the purchase

HOW TO REACH AFFINITY GROUPS

There is no formula for reaching out to membership organizations, so it is up to you to be creative in searching them out. Start with the nonprofit fine arts and cultural organizations in your community, such as museums, zoos, or historical societies. Most of these organizations employ a membership director whose job it is to develop membership and reinforce affinity.

If you are a producer of a show with a particular theme, seek out national membership organizations or charities that have some organic connection. Pitch the executive national leadership of the charity so that every chapter can have an event in its city when the tour arrives there.

Contact the alumni affairs offices at the top twenty-five colleges and universities and get the local chapter contacts for your city.

Invite these folks to your next show and pitch them on doing annual alumni events.

Go to Google™ and type the name of your city with the word *chapter* (i.e. "Atlanta chapter"). This will give you an instant list of affinity organizations. And that's just the start. You can find extraordinary information about membership organizations on the local, regional, and national level by simply searching under different criteria or accessing listing resources.

In short, any organization with members is fair game. All it takes is finding the decision maker and pitching a theatre party plan that best fits his/her needs.

TIPS FOR SUCCESS WITH AFFINITY GROUPS

Dig deep and contact the right decision makers. Be persuasive and be ready to follow through. Be creative and willing to inspire membership and/or development directors with your vision.

Reach out to the right people for the right show. Make concise pitches that spell out exactly why it is in their interest to hold a member event in conjunction with the show. Take the ones who show interest and run with them. Don't waste time trying to convince someone who is resistant; there are too many opportunities to bother with those who can't see the potential.

Have a "how to" package of information prepared for people who like the idea but aren't sure how to go about planning such an event. Spell out exactly how to plan and execute a membership event or theatre party. If you are unsure what the steps are, contact someone who has done one and ask for their advice.

Consider developing a bundled singles booking mechanism. What stops most large-scale events is the issue of who's going to manage all that money and distribute all those tickets. If they can have their members call you for their exclusive group tickets and you can keep the individual price below the public consumer rate, you'll be prepared to open the door to numerous, custom-made large group opportunities.

Think big. Start by selling the entire house. Many potential group buyers don't know they can buy an entire performance. Focus on big organizations that do annual events. Stay focused on the larger events and quickly pass the small groups on to your processing staff.

Have fun. Take some of the time you save by not having to sell all those seats one bus at a time and help your buyout customers put together a great event.

Group Leaders

Category:	Business-to-Business Business-to-Consumer
Sub-markets:	Professional Group Activity Coordinators Group Travel Planners Consumer Group Leaders

PROFESSIONAL GROUP ACTIVITY COORDINATORS

Professional group activity coordinators organize group activities as part of their jobs. Some work for senior centers and adult living communities; some work for public agencies and local communities; some work in-house for corporations and businesses; some work for banks to plan activities for depositors; and some work for schools. These people are professionals who are charged with seeking out and providing quality group entertainment for the various populations served by their employers.

GROUP TRAVEL PLANNERS

Group travel planners are quasi-professionals who coordinate group activities in exchange for free travel or other forms of cash or in-kind compensation. The group travel industry has begun distinguishing group travel planners and recognizing them for the power and influence they wield in deciding where to direct group dollars.

GROUP LEADERS

Group leaders are non-professionals who organize travel and other group activities for their peers. They are often but not always senior citizens. Group leaders tend to be the people in the organization who have the energy, the inclination, and the time to put together group outings. They are generally better motivated than their peers, and they stay up on what travel and entertainment opportunities are available to groups.

These three categories constitute the bulk of most entertainment-related group sales databases. They are the bread and butter of the group sales efforts of most venues, and they remain a productive source of sales. They are the people most entertainment industry professionals think of when they think about group buyers and they are the people the group sales business model was designed to accommodate.

Thought of collectively as *group leaders,* these three buyer types flock to live entertainment because they are pre-motivated to select group activities that appeal to their constituents and because they are often personally interested in seeing the shows.

WHAT GROUP LEADERS NEED

- Advance information on show schedules

- Service appropriate for professionals who work with groups

- Information about the show so they can communicate effectively with their people

- Information about other group services and attractions in the venue neighborhood

- Marketing materials

- Complimentary tickets or other creative and appropriate incentives for their bookings

HOW TO REACH GROUP LEADERS

Your group sales database is the best possible source to locate these buyers. Otherwise ask others in your community who sell similar group products or compatible group services. Their databases will contain names yours does not, so consider some sort of win-win cooperative sales initiative.

Outbound calling is the best way to stay in touch with your group leader clientele. There is significant turnover in this market, so it is a good idea to clean your list by calling to find out who has taken over if the group contact has changed. A lot of these group leaders are seniors, after all, so they can't stay at it forever.

Some professional group buyers are affiliated with trade associations such as Group Leaders of America (GLAMER) or Banktravel.com. Many others will subscribe to publications such as *Leisure Group Travel, Group Tour Magazine, The Group Travel Leader,* or *Bank Travel Management,* to name a few. Most of these organizations and/or publishers offer marketing services targeted to group travel planners, group leaders in your area, or remote buyers who plan travel to your destination.

Everybody needs to rent buses so your local motor coach charter services will have the most comprehensive lists of group leaders in your region. Meet with the charter companies in your area and offer to pay them to mail your collateral to their proprietary customer lists. Suggest that they promote their charter service along with the show so they will see the win-win potential. Be prepared to discuss access and parking. Every group seller has to deal with these issues at one time or another.

TIPS FOR SUCCESS WITH GROUPS LEADERS

Take a close look at your group sales database and try to subdivide your group leaders into professionals, travel planners and consumer group leaders. Know who buys what and think about various motivating factors when planning your group sales campaigns.

Get to know your local and regional activity coordinators personally. Join your local corporate employee services association such as Employee Services Management Association (ESM). Look for local or regional organizations of activity directors or geriatric support services professionals. Network with these people and learn how you can best meet their needs.

Tailor programs for your corporate employee services contacts. Consider bundling singles or exclusive employee nights.

Learn what motivates group leaders and use that to stimulate business. If the promise of free "driver and escort" tickets puts you ahead of the competition, the increase in group sales will more than cover the cost of the incentive comps.

Identify which group buyers on your list qualify as group travel planners. Give them a higher priority than group leaders and offer them unique incentives for working with you.

Make sure your day-trip and domestic long-haul tour operators receive complimentary tickets for each group they book so they can incentivize the planners who buy from them.

Keep and nurture every customer you get. If you lose one, make sure you find out who is replacing him or her because if you lose the group leader, you lose the group.

Charities

Category:	Business-to-Business
Markets:	Fundraising Managers and Volunteer Leaders

Charities are always looking for interesting ways to raise money. When it comes to stage entertainment, some charities will organize large fund-raisers or "theatre parties" in conjunction with the opening of a show. These generally entail a large block of tickets and a pre- or post-show party. Others will secure blocks of tickets to sell to their donors at a marked-up price.

Charities prefer to have theatre parties at the beginning of a run so they can advertise priority access to their potential donors. They tend to prefer shows that will be popular or distinctive so there will be some exclusivity to their event. Most will need access to nearby party venues for pre- or post-show events. Theatre parties are often large groups of three or four hundred to full houses.

Charities target affluent donors who are generally influential community leaders. Having a high profile charity event in the first or second performance can start word of mouth about a show spreading in extremely desirable markets. Theatre parties can be great PR for a show that appeals to the moneyed elite, but a theatre party can have the opposite effect on a show that appeals to a different market. You'll want to match your charity and show carefully.

It is easier and more profitable to sell one full venue than to sell the same number of seats thirty-five tickets at a time. Buyouts and large group theatre parties are the most cost effective ways of moving ticket inventory. Charities secure large blocks of tickets and mobilize external sales teams in highly desirable target markets. Yes, they do take some hand holding, but good charity clients can be dependable sources of large group sales year after year.

Planning for theatre parties means keeping a few dates open at the beginning of the run so charities have access to the best dates. Packing early performances full of subscribers can prevent hundreds of thousands of dollars in large group sales and whole-house buy-outs.

Some charities prefer to obtain their own tickets to popular shows and sell them at a markup to their constituents. Consignment programs and limited-risk group sales can mobilize large armies of volunteer ticket sellers in hard-to-penetrate markets.

WHAT CHARITIES NEED

- Advance information on show schedules with complete date ranges (even if they are not advertised to local single ticket buyers)

- National charities will need complete details about national tour schedules to coordinate local chapters' fundraising strategies

- Priority access to large blocks of tickets in early performances

- Flexible payment policies with incremental due dates to lessen risk

- Information about the show so they can communicate effectively with their people

- Marketing materials

- An ongoing relationship with the group seller

- Assistance with services for large on-site or nearby parties

HOW TO REACH CHARITIES

Keep an eye on your community's social calendar or the society pages of your major daily paper. Learn what charitable organizations hold which galas and fundraisers at what time of year. Collect commemorative programs from these events and learn who the key figures are who plan the events and oversee their execution. Make a target list of the fundraising executives and volunteer community leaders. Make sure they are all on your database and coded as VIP charity contacts.

A little research on the web will help you find major foundations and public grantors that give money to charities and non-profit organizations in your community. Most are required to make their grant recipients public so you can easily obtain a comprehensive list of grant recipients in your community. The relative size of grants can be an indication of the size of the charities. The larger ones are better equipped to plan and execute elaborate stage entertainment-related galas.

Once you have honed down your list, contact the executive director, development director, or key volunteer leader (board chair or board president) of your top targets. Pitch them the idea of having their next major fundraising event in conjunction with an upcoming show.

Don't forget catering companies and event planners. These are often the people called upon to provide the ideas for gala fundraisers. Stay in close contact and give them the information they need to pitch fundraising event ideas that include your upcoming shows.

Zero in on a handful of major charitable organizations—ones that don't compete against one another for the same contributors, if possible—and nurture relationships that will play out in several annual theatre party galas for years to come.

TIPS FOR SUCCESS WITH CHARITIES

Be ready to help by providing access to resources but avoid getting sucked in to the planning process. Fundraisers are experts at getting people to do things for them. They may ask for some kind of price break or charitable donation from you! Be firm on what you can and cannot offer and don't waste time with buyers who have unreasonable expectations about ticket prices and access to artists or the venue's or producer's resources.

Put together a how-to manual with lists of vendors so that people who haven't done a theatre party can handle it. The resources you list should be cooperative partners who have an interest in working with you to make these events successful and productive for all parties.

Have a theatre party contract drafted that enables you to collect payments in increments to minimize risk to you and your charitable client. Most charities won't absorb risks by paying large sums up front.

Create a cooperative plan for selling theatre parties with your caterer or venue sales rep. Their lists of sales contacts will augment yours.

Be professional. People who plan gala fund-raisers are often leaders in the business community. Your professionalism can go a long way toward tipping the decision making in your favor.

Educators

Category:	Business-to-Business
	Business-to-Consumer

Educators buy theatre tickets for student groups. Their motives range from statewide educational mandates to an individual teacher's interest in seeing a particular show. Many decisions are made by dedicated teachers who go out of their way to arrange arts and entertainment experiences for their kids. In general, educators are professionals who purchase arts and entertainment tickets as a function of their jobs, but many of the buying decisions are driven by the consumer tastes and motivations of individual teachers.

Educators tend to want low-priced tickets on weekday matinees, although price-sensitivity will vary widely by school district. Student groups can also be convened for evening or weekend performances. The willingness to plan outside the school day or academic calendar is often dependent on the motivation of the individual educator and the relative affluence of the school community. Few inner-city systems are set up to accommodate such extracurricular opportunities.

From a revenue perspective, students are not full-price buyers but they can be profitable sources of ticket sales. Managing the yield from student groups relative to adult buyers can keep houses full and generate revenue when seats might otherwise go empty.

Student groups are the best way to reach tomorrow's arts and entertainment audience. Providing access for student groups is an invaluable long-term audience development strategy for both commercial and not-for-profit arts and stage entertainment providers. Commercial producers, however, have short-term revenue goals that can prevent them from investing in long-range audience development.

Educational outreach programs vary. Commercial entertainment companies can have elaborate educational initiatives that are designed to drive ticket sales while not-for-profit organizations can have equally elaborate programs designed to expose kids to performance events and fill seats. It is up to each group sales professional to understand how the sales mission of his or her organization relates to the educational mission and to develop priorities accordingly. Sales departments should be prepared to draw a specific line between sales and outreach, however, or they can become buried in not-for-profit mission-oriented activities that detract from strategic sales objectives.

Conversely, in many organizations there can be significant gaps between revenue-driven group sales initiatives and genuine educational outreach. Closing these gaps can often result in more dynamic group sales programs that combine credible educational content with legitimate earnings potential and audience development.

WHAT EDUCATORS NEED

- Advance information on show schedules with complete date ranges, even if they are not advertised to local single-ticket buyers

- Booking windows that fit into academic budgeting calendars

- Payment policies that fit with educational/governmental infrastructures

- Information about the show so they can communicate effectively with their students

- Study guides to help work the show into educational curricula

- Access to programs that add educational value to the arts and entertainment experience

- Marketing materials

- An ongoing relationship with the group seller

HOW TO REACH EDUCATORS

School markets are huge so it helps to prioritize your database contacts. Start by grade range; for example, first through third, fourth through sixth, middle school, high school, college, adult ed. Then look at the relative affluence of systems. Educators in more affluent systems tend to be better motivated and have an easier time collecting payments. Less affluent systems may contain more deserving kids, however, and they may be more appropriate targets for organizations with educational outreach mandates.

Prioritize your contacts, too. Start with your database and divide your existing educational contacts by system administrators, curriculum developers, principals, department heads, performing arts faculty, to name a few. If the show has inherent appeal to one particular discipline, single out the teachers who teach that subject. If the show appeals to a specific demographic category, make sure to code those educators appropriately as well.

When looking for ways to expand your educational outreach, start with the leaders in the systems you plan to target. Forging relationships with key curriculum developers or school system administrators can smooth the way for communicating with the individuals who make the decisions to book the groups. If the systems you are targeting have overarching educational mandates that fit with your group sales objectives, coordinate your efforts with your organization's education department for more effective outreach.

If your market contains underserved student populations who should be attending your shows, consider reaching out to corporate underwriters who will buy the tickets on behalf of deserving students. Some corporate underwriters will welcome the opportunity to give the tickets as long as the school or venue can take care of the logistics and the underwriter can brag about having made the access possible.

TIPS FOR SUCCESS WITH EDUCATORS

Pay close attention to your statewide curriculum guidelines. If your show or your educational program fits within the guidelines, you'll have a more active market of teachers and administrators.

Obtain copies of study guides or educational support materials as early as possible and meet with the curriculum developers to make sure the lessons are integrated into the school year early enough to be meaningful. If you can identify a group of key educators who have an interest in a given show, consider convening a workshop to introduce the study guide and discuss how the show can meet the system's educational objectives.

Coordinate visiting artist and speaker bureaus to make sure their outreach is compatible with your group sales marketing. Work with your education department to develop sales campaigns that fit in with their initiatives.

Consider a "teacher rush" program that offers low-cost, last minute tickets. Pitch it as a familiarization (FAM) opportunity and capture names and addresses for your database. Otherwise, make sure that your top-level administrators are on your VIP invitation list and that you invite them whenever your organization is papering. Be selective about inviting teachers, however, as some buy groups so they can see a particular show. Inviting them for a preview may dampen their enthusiasm for coming back with their kids. (Alas, it is true.)

Be sensitive to educational calendars and financial infrastructures. You'll want to promote shows when systems are planning curricula and while budgets are being planned. And don't forget that many systems work on a purchase order system that may require flexible payment terms.

SMERFs

Category:	Business-to-Consumer

Sub-markets:	Social Groups
	Military Groups
	Ethnic Groups
	Religious Groups
	Fraternal Groups

The SMERF designation (notice initial letters above) comes from the hotel industry where it helps to separate lower revenue consumer groups from more profitable B-to-B clientele. The stage entertainment industry may depend more on SMERFs than the hospitality industry, but the model is instructive for several reasons:

- Our traditional take-whatever-comes-our-way attitude toward groups has loaded us with SMERFs to the exclusion of more profitable B-to-B customers

- Pulling SMERFs out of the market mix helps to identify other, more productive target markets

- Pulling SMERFs out of the market mix also helps us understand the dynamics of SMERF sub-markets apart from more business-oriented buyers

- The SMERF designation further reinforces the importance of B-to-B versus B-to-C methods

There is significant crossover between the group leader category and SMERFs. It is fair to say that most SMERF groups are organized by individuals who can reasonably be called group leaders. But group leader has a distinct senior connotation and isn't sufficient to cover the diversity of consumer group buyers represented among SMERF clientele.

SOCIAL GROUPS

Social groups typically consist of friends, peers and family members. A social group event is put together by an enterprising individual consumer, and can be centered on a special occasion or shared interest in live entertainment or the content of a specific show. Social groups can be customers who book regularly, but they also book spontaneously to do something special or take advantage of a group incentive. Spontaneous social group bookers may have little long-term interest in coordinating group activity so they are often one-off customers.

MILITARY GROUPS

Military groups are self-explanatory. They will be important to venues within a reasonable commute of military installations. The groups typically consist of military personnel and their families. The decision makers tend to be spouses or personnel who organize group activity as a part of their assignments.

ETHNIC GROUPS

Ethnic groups is a designation that applies—somewhat unfairly—to demographic categories that we may target for a specific show. Within any ethnic category, however, you will find all buyer types outlined in this book. For this section, ethnic groups refers to *consumer* groups with a specific cultural interest in a given entertainment provider or show.

RELIGIOUS GROUPS

Religious groups are people who attend the churches, synagogues and mosques that appear on all group sales lists. These are essentially social groups who convene within a religious community setting. Otherwise, they are subgroups in a church such as choirs, youth ministries, senior groups, or auxiliaries. Traditional church-going habits are changing in the U.S. and Canada with fewer young people joining and participating in their parents' main-line congregations. It remains to be seen if the newer mega-church phenomenon will deliver group buyers to theatrical events. If it does, show content will be an important factor.

FRATERNAL GROUPS

Fraternal groups are Masons, Lions, Elks, Greeks, Rotarians, Knights of Columbus, Daughters of Isis, and innumerable other local brotherhoods, sisterhoods, orders, associations, and special interest or community groups. These groups gather periodically to engage in some sort of ritual activity and most embrace a human service cause for which they raise money or provide support services. They are usually marked by exclusivity or a secret societal culture knowable only to the initiated. Like churches, fraternal organizations are experiencing a falling-off in participation among younger generations suggesting that their group sales potential will diminish in years to come.

We target SMERFs because they are organized communities who engage in group activity on a regular basis. They are part of a culture that accepts belonging to groups as a part of what it means to participate in their society. It is a culture on the wane, however, so SMERFs should be courted only as a part of a broader market mix.

WHAT SMERFs NEED

- Advance information on show schedules with as much information on availability as can be communicated publicly

- Incentives that may tip a smaller group or family into the official group category

- Information about the show so they can communicate effectively with their people

- Advertising messages that motivate potential group buyers

HOW TO REACH SMERFs

Existing group sales databases are the best possible sources for finding consumer groups. Start by identifying the SMERFs on your database and coding them appropriately. If you cannot assign an accurate code, call them, tell them what you are doing, and ask how they would like to be coded. Be careful how you assign codes to ethnic groups, however.

Partner with other group sales professionals in your region — especially the ones who sell to local groups. Create win-win cooperative promotions so that you can gain access to their databases.

Advertise group availability and incentives aggressively in all single-ticket advertising. Work with your marketing department to make sure the group message is not only prominent in the ads but that it is *persuasive* as well. If you have a group discount, say it. If you can mention a reason to book a group, all the better: "Makes a great group outing for any organization. Visit www.buygroupstoday.com for details on discounts and incentives. Or call 1-800-555-1234."

TIPS FOR SUCCESS WITH SMERFs

Organize your database by SMERF category and be specific when you contact those customers. Understand what motivates them to buy and give them all the reasons they need to decide in your favor.

Be a good and willing cooperative partner with other group sales professionals and charter bus companies in your community. SMERFs are consumers who respond mostly to consumer advertising, so they are hard to find through pre-existing marketing channels. The best way to find them is through others who maintain proprietary customer lists that also contain SMERFs.

Hold on to them when you get them! Give them the best possible customer service and keep your SMERF customers happy so they'll come back often.

Group Markets Overview

Here then are the primary market breakdowns:

MEETINGS AND INCENTIVES (B-to-B)

Meeting planners, DMCs, event planners, and incentive professionals are the corporate group buyers who deal mostly with gatherings of business people from out of town. Count on them for large groups, whole-house buyouts, and top dollar bookings.

DOMESTIC GROUP TOUR OPERATORS (B-to-B)

Whether they're coming from across town or across the continent, tour groups love stage entertainment. Establish strong relationships with these loyal, repeat tour operator customers and they'll deliver high volume purchases for seniors, students, and traveling groups of all kinds.

CORPORATIONS AND BUSINESSES (B-to-B)

Local businesses buy tickets to entertain clients and reward employees. The individuals who do the buying may be hard to find, but the enormous potential is worth the effort.

INTERNATIONAL TRAVEL MARKETS (B-to-B)

They're not for everyone but international tour operators, wholesalers, and receptive operators can be a boon to venues in popular destination cities that offer shows with international appeal.

STRATEGIC SELLING PARTNERS (B-to-B)

Group events are package affairs so selling your product in a vacuum is extremely shortsighted. Go out and partner with all the other folks who do what you do in your community. You'll grow your own business and help to grow the overall groups market for your destination.

AFFINITY ORGANIZATIONS (B-to-B)

If the organization has members, it's fair game. Find all the membership group organizers in your market, or those who coordinate events in your market, and convince them to do an event or special offer in conjunction with your shows.

GROUP LEADERS (B-to-B, B-to-C)

Hey, watch who you're calling a group leader! These folks coordinate groups for their organizations. Some are paid, some get informal perks, and some do it because they're more motivated than others.

CHARITIES (B-to-B)

Theatre party fundraisers are big, top-dollar events that draw valuable opinion leaders into early performances. How many large non-profit organizations are there in your market? If you are a producer, is there a national charity that should be doing a major event in every city on your tour schedule?

EDUCATORS (B-to-B, B-to-C)

Targeting educators in an organized fashion will enable you to sell more student groups and help you integrate educational initiatives with sales objectives. It's not top-dollar business, but the volume can make up for the diminished revenue.

SMERFs (B-to-C)

Think about the various motivations that influence sales from among your B-to-C buyers. Social, military, ethnic, religious and fraternal groups all have different needs and expectations so speak to these individual needs.

It is important to understand that group buyers are increasingly business buyers who need businesslike services. It is also vital to understand how buyers' businesses function so you can persuade them to buy and then meet their needs in the most efficient manner.

Now that you know who they are, go get them!

PART III

THE METHODS

This section is primarily intended for group sales professionals but it is useful information for the managers and executive leaders who oversee their work.

Any group sales professional who follows these recommendations, whether entirely or in part, cannot help but improve his or her sales. Any organization that embraces these methods and supports the group department's efforts to put them to work will lower costs and increase productivity.

Plan

Every sales initiative should begin with a strategic plan that spells out exactly what is to be accomplished. Some organizations will be familiar with long-range planning and some will find the concept foreign and perhaps intimidating. Commercial theatre, for example, is so steeped in risk and uncertainty that the idea of long-range planning is to some unthinkable.

I had a friend in New York who was always hitting me up to "invest" in his Off-Broadway projects. He'd say, "Hey, Trev, how about putting ten thousand into my new show?" I'd say, "Send me a marketing plan." He'd say, "That's ridiculous. This is theatre. We don't do marketing plans before the show opens." I'd say, "When you show me that you've thought about how many tickets you're going to sell from the minute the show goes on sale through the first six months of your run—and how you're going to sell them—you can have my ten thousand dollars." It was the safest promise I could make and it never cost me a cent because theatrical producers back then were often artists and gamblers who became businessmen only if their shows survived the vagaries of public tastes and critical reviews.

Now, of course, stage entertainment is increasingly the product of corporate interests, institutional producers, and presenting organizations where strategic planning plays an important role. It remains to be seen how much of this strategic thinking is making its way into group sales, but if it's not, the following guidelines should offer a reasonably good place to start.

A good plan will include answers to these questions:

WHAT ARE YOUR OVERALL OBJECTIVES?

The difference between goals and objectives is subtle but important. In general, objectives are accomplishments, such as increasing sales or reorganizing priorities, whereas goals are end points such as total dollars or total tickets sold.

The best way to clarify objectives is to say, "By the end of this campaign we will have _____," then fill in the blank with all the things you intend to accomplish:

Example:

- ... exceeded the previous year's sales by fifteen percent

- ... reorganized the department for more emphasis on outbound sales

- ... reached out to three major new untapped markets

- ... added one hundred new B-to-B buyers to the client roster

To turn them into objectives, simply restate them in the future tense by removing the 'ed':

Example:

Campaign Objectives:

By the end of the campaign, we will:

- ... exceed the previous year's sales by fifteen percent

- ... reorganize the department for more emphasis on outbound sales

- ... reach out to three major new untapped markets

- … add one hundred new B-to-B buyers to the client roster

Stating objectives gives you a clear sense of what you are supposed to have done when you finish. When your campaign is over, you'll be able to revisit these objectives and determine whether or not you did what you set out to do.

WHAT ARE YOUR GOALS?
Goals are usually the sales numbers you intend to reach.

Example:

- Overall goal: $2.5 million and 45,500 tickets

- Sales to existing clients: $2 million

- Incremental sales to new clients: $500k

Goals should be based on such factors as past performance, relative desirability of the product, and projections attached to every campaign described in the strategic plan. Naturally, you'll want to set these goals collaboratively with your general manager and marketing team to make certain they fit within the overall audience development scheme.

WHAT MARKETS WILL YOU REACH OUT TO?
Your research should help you identify which new markets are worth targeting, so your plan should identify which markets you plan to approach. It is a good idea to attach reasonable goals to each market even if you aren't exactly sure how an unfamiliar market will perform.

Attaching goals to target markets is a process of using historical sales data, experience, expertise, and intuition to guess how many sales each market will deliver. If you lack the necessary tools, get help from someone who has them. Projections will always be guesses, but you'll want to base them on as much objective and/or authoritative information as you can find.

Example:

MARKET BY MARKET GOALS

Meeting Planners	= 1 buyout for 2,200 tickets	@ $130k
DMCs	= 3 groups for 250 tickets	@ $18k
Day-Trip Tour Operators	= 20 groups for 800 tickets	@ $50k
Local Businesses	= 10 groups for 500 tickets	@ $35k

After you've attached a goal to each sub-market, add them up to arrive at your total goal.

WHAT STRATEGIC MESSAGES WILL YOU BE USING FOR EACH MARKET?

This is one of the most important steps but it is often overlooked. Take the time to spell out exactly what the strategic message will be for every target market. It can be as simple as a list of selling points based on the unique needs of each market segment.

Example:

Tour Operators

- Attractive group discounts

- New senior seating in orchestra

- New elevators to balcony for more price-sensitive groups

- Flexible payment terms for buyers of six groups or more

- Great incentives, such as gift with purchase and driver and escort comps

- Three out of five shows this season are extremely popular with groups

- Merchandise discount vouchers with each group of forty or more

- Convenient drop off with optional meet and greet

- Convenient motor coach parking

- Excellent local restaurant packages for convenient, affordable dining

- Early curtain times for students/seniors who need to be home early

- Hotel discounts at nearby Marriott

Having these messages spelled out in advance will help you develop all your targeted sales materials, and they will give you the persuasive language you need for your in-person sales meetings.

WHAT VEHICLES WILL YOU BE USING TO DELIVER THOSE STRATEGIC MESSAGES?

The next natural step is to describe the tools you need to communicate these persuasive messages to your target markets:

Example:

Student Youth Tour Operators

- Co-op package mailing with Hard Rock Café

- Join SYTA/attend annual conference

- Join the state Activities Directors Association and attend their annual conference

- Call three names from target lists every week

- Prepare visiting student brochure and distribute it through

    Convention and Visitors Bureau

    Natural History Museum sales department

    Zoo sales department

    Space Center sales department

    University summer housing sales office

    Partner hotel sales teams

    Mail to NTA/SYTA members

WHAT TIMELINE WILL GOVERN THE OUTREACH?

After you have outlined the messages and the media, organize your activities into a master calendar that plots each event and backs out the significant deadlines leading to them.

Example:

SYTA/Hard Rock Co-op Mailer Timeline:

Drop date:	March 26
Printed piece delivered to mail house:	March 22
Mail lists to mail house:	March 19
Final approved art/copy to print:	March 5
First draft from designer:	February 20
Final copy/photos/logos to designer:	February 13
Projections to GM:	February 10
Strategy/creative meeting:	February 6

Once you have done this for each of the principal initiatives in your plan, transfer the dates to a master calendar. Once all the dates are in the master calendar, you will have a clear sense of where major deadlines fall and what you'll need to do every day to stay on schedule.

Example:

Monday, April 14

- Deadline for copy for spring SMERF mailer

- Registration deadline for SYTA conference is next Friday

- Lunch meeting with HR director at XYZ Corp.

- Schools mailer drops for fall/winter performances

- New staff incentives go into effect

- Sales calls/schedule appointments with: Gotham School District arts curriculum head, owner of Creative Concepts Party Planners, American Cancer Society chapter head; Notre Dame alumni chapter head

- Draft memo to BO and GM regarding new 24-hour confirmations

- Review final web-booking pages before Friday launch

- CVB mixer 6:00 tonight at Wyndham Hotel

A fully plotted master calendar will tell you exactly what you should be working on at any given moment. Real life will keep the plan from working perfectly, but having a plan in writing makes you aware of how far ahead or behind you are relative to your strategic objectives and sales projections.

HOW MUCH MONEY DO YOU PLAN TO SPEND ON EACH INITIATIVE?

Defining your targets and outlining your methods will give you the raw material you need to create your budget. Attaching costs to each initiative will enable you to back into your overall totals.

Example:

GROUP SALES BUDGET DETAIL

In-House database Mailer 1
(Generic season "Early Bird" drops April 10 to 15,000 names)

Design	$ 1,000
Print	$ 2,000
Mail house	$ 750
Postage	$ 2,850
Mailer 1 Subtotal	**$ 6,600**

Often group sales budgets are determined by what the organization wants to spend. "Here's your budget. Tell me how you plan to spend it." The more efficient way is to figure out how many tickets you can reasonably sell and then back into an appropriate dollar amount by asking yourself, "How much will I have to spend to sell this many tickets?" If you've done your homework, you can defend your budget by demonstrating that it is based on reasonable assumptions about potential yield. Ultimately, your budget will be a compromise between what your organization wants to spend, or has traditionally spent, and what your well-supported estimates will have targeted.

HOW MANY TICKETS AND DOLLARS IS EACH CAMPAIGN EXPECTED TO DELIVER?

It is a good idea to get into the habit of projecting results for each sales initiative. If you are going to drop a fifteen thousand-piece mailer to your in-house database, you'll need a clear understanding of how that mailer is expected to return. Take the time to estimate how many of those fifteen thousand recipients will respond to the mailer, how many tickets they will buy, and how much money they will spend.

Example:

GROUP SALES PROJECTION DETAIL

NUMBER CONTACTS	RESPONSE RATE	NUMBER RESPONSES	AVERAGE TIX PER	TOTAL TIX	AVERAGE $ PER TICKET	TOTAL DOLLARS	COST TO MAIL
15,000	0.80%	120	35	4200	$57.00	$239,400	$6,600.00

If you do this for each initiative in your plan, you will know:

- How much money is coming in relative to what you are spending

- What goals each campaign must reach in order to be considered cost-effective

- How many tickets your overall strategic plan is estimated to yield

- How much money your strategic plan is estimated to bring in

Projections are not always accurate but your best educated guess is always better than "we'll see what happens." The process you go through to come up with reasonable guesses and the before-the-fact analyses will help you know whether a given campaign is worth launching. As you implement and assess your strategic plan, you will learn to refine the accuracy of your future projections. In the long run, you'll develop increasingly precise predictions based on a combination of quantitative analyses, accumulated knowledge, and more precise intuition.

HOW WILL YOU MODIFY PLANS IF THE SITUATION CHANGES?

In live entertainment and performing arts, plans never work out the way they're supposed to. That's why so many arts and entertainment professionals neglect the planning process in the first place.

Knowing that a plan won't work ahead of time, however, gives you an opportunity to decide what to do differently. Will you cut advertising in a certain publication if it doesn't work? By what date? How many months are you willing to invest in a cold-calling campaign for local businesses before pulling the plug? What will you do if one of the shows is canceled? Where will you trim if sales are only at seventy-five percent of your mid-year goal?

Understanding that change is inevitable, you can save a lot of grief by having a Plan B available. No plan will be perfect and every plan will need to be altered. Even if your plan goes out the window altogether, you will be better off for having made one. At least you will know where you were heading so you can figure out what to do to get back on track.

The simple act of developing a plan can give structure to sales activity, which might have progressed without form or purpose.

Learn

There are, no doubt, other businesses in your market that court group buyers. Some may do it better than you do, some may do it in a more commercial arena, some may target different geographical markets, some may sell products that differ from yours, and some may compete directly against you. Every community large enough to have a professional entertainment venue or host a professional stage event usually has hotels, attractions, and services that market themselves to groups.

This means that there are group sales professionals in your market who are dealing with your same issues and who may be working with customers you have yet to reach. Among them are smart, accomplished, professional salespeople who are worth knowing. Your job is to go out and find the people in your market who do what you do, meet with them on a regular basis, find out to which associations and business networks they belong, join those associations and networks, and begin interacting regularly with your colleagues. Listen to them, learn from them, share with them and develop industry relationships that will serve you throughout your career.

Then go to the destination marketing organizations that support your efforts such as convention and visitors bureaus, chambers of commerce, government tourism agencies, and regional sales and marketing collectives. Seek out the professionals who deal with group sales and pick their brains. Find out who can help you most and stay close. Join the organizations that offer the most valuable support and get everything you can out of your memberships.

Seek out trade associations where your customers do business. From Group Leaders of America (GLAMER) to the Travel Industry Association of America (TIA), nearly every professional group buyer type is connected with a trade association that allows you to access similar customers. Learn how to maximize business with their members. That's what these associations are there to do.

Speak to your customers. Meet them in their offices; learn their businesses; find out what they need from you to make their relationships with you more productive. Learn how to offer the most valuable services to them, even if it means changing decades-old traditions and box office operations.

Find a consultant with expertise in group sales and ask him/her for professional advice. Find someone who has done what you do in a different market and ask for help in planning more efficient sales initiatives. Get practical advice on your strategic plan before you spend too much time or money on the wrong things.

Create relationships with your local group sales colleagues and ask for advice. It takes a certain amount of humility but most group salespeople love being asked, and veterans in the commercial group sales arena are generally very decent, helpful people. It is a service profession after all, so the ones who do it well are usually very accommodating.

Get out into your professional group sales arena and start learning from your peers!

Organize

The most important sales and marketing tool for group sales is a well-organized database of active buyers. These are your existing customers and potential new customers, so it is extremely important to be able to communicate with them in an organized, meaningful manner.

Your database should include a carefully coded, searchable list of buyers who have purchased groups from you within the last three to five years. It should also include names of carefully selected potential customers that have been coded as speculative contacts. In addition to the names you own and control, your data universe should include all external databases that are *potentially* available to you through cooperative sales initiatives with strategic partners in your community.

Customer data is the foundation of your sales effort and the most efficient tool you have for managing relationships with your buyers. Marketing and sales initiatives are crucial for expanding your numbers but their ultimate goal is to add names to your family of loyal repeat customers. If it is ten times more expensive to get a new customer than to keep an old one, you'll want to make sure your customer information is as accurate and useful as possible.

EXISTING DATA

If you haven't coded your database yet, do it now. Sort your entire database by buyer type according to the breakdowns in this book. You may find that your data can be sorted into even more detailed categories within each major heading. The more criteria you use to sort your data, the more efficient your group sales marketing will be.

When this process is finished, assign codes to the different buyer types and subcategories. Your ability to code and categorize your data will be determined by the database program you are using. A good system will enable you to assign multiple codes and to sort the data in many different ways. More robust systems will enable you to sort by buyer type together with sales history. Ideally, you'll want to be able to pull up a customer profile that looks something like this:

Ms. Storm Cloud
Storm Cloud Gatherings
123 Rainey Lane
Suite #456
Tacoma, WA 78910
123-456-7891 (t.)
123-456-7890 (f.)
scloud@stormcloudgatherings.net

Buyer Type:	DMC (Destination Management Company)
Location:	LOC (Local)
Family:	MPL (Meeting Planners) INC (Incentive) CRP (Corporate)
History:	STP (Stomp) CDS (Cirque du Soleil) DOI (Disney on Ice)
Three Yr. Cume:	$155,000

THE BUYER TYPE is your primary designation. Most customers will fit neatly into a single category. If they don't, select the category that fits best. If you can, assign subordinate categories within this heading.

THE LOCATION is your geographical designation. Sometimes you'll want to pull a list of the closest buyers for a short turn-around special deal that only your nearest buyers can enjoy. Other times you'll want to send long-lead announcements only to your remote customers so they can plan in advance. If you have good zip sorting capabilities, this can do the same thing.

THE FAMILY designation refers to buyer types that fit together within certain broader categories. There will be times when you want to send something to all buyers within a certain family such as MICE or SMERFs and this makes it easier to pull them all together.

HISTORY is where you'll record the data about what each customer has purchased. This won't necessarily be easy and sometimes you'll need to cross-reference against box office records to match purchase history against other data. Obviously, there will be occasions where knowing what purchases a client has made will be extremely useful.

THREE YEAR CUME is also more complex. Only the most sophisticated programs will enable you to attach a cumulative spend to each record, but it is possible. Ultimately, this is the standard you'll want to work toward because knowing the spending history of your customers is vital to understanding their long-term value.

If your group sales database is not tied into your box office system or if it is not a strong enough marketing tool, get a new one. If you can't wait for your box office to modernize, get a better group sales data storage and retrieval system and run parallel programs until you can reintegrate. If your box office is more sophisticated than you are, get up to their level ASAP. There is no excuse for not knowing your clientele and not being able to pull lists from your database according to specific criteria.

If, perish the thought, your data is poorly organized in the computer, but available to you in old boxes full of paper orders, take the time to re-build the list. The cost of typing in a few thousand records is nothing compared to the benefits of having a clean, accurate, well-organized database.

If you have a large quantity of contacts that cannot be identified by buyer type or sales history, call them, explain what you are doing and ask them how they want to be listed. Calling customers to tell them you are improving your systems is excellent customer service and it will probably stimulate some sales. Commercial organizations can do this despite recent Do Not Call laws if the contact has a purchase history. Not-for-profits should be able to call without violating any laws. If you are unsure, check with your lawyers.

If you have buyer names that are three years old with no intervening sales history, call them to find out if they are still active. If you have no phone numbers, look them up on a good search engine or an online Yellow Pages and track them down. If you can't find them, mail them a notice explaining that you are cleaning your list and they should call or drop an email if they want to continue getting your information. If they don't respond, take them off the list. No sense in wasting time on non-responsive contacts.

NEW MARKETS

After your own data is in order, start looking at new markets to determine which ones are right for the products you want to sell. Your list will tell you a lot about which markets have been interested in the past. Looking at what's *not* on your list will show you where you might want to go in the future. Take the buyer types outlined in this book, compare them against your database, find out who is missing, and start going after the ones who show the most promise.

If your database is the core of your group sales marketing effort, you will want to begin expanding it with carefully selected external databases that contain potential new customers. Here are some suggestions for adding speculative names to your existing list:

Every trade association you join will have a database of buyer members and most will offer you an opportunity to sort that list to narrow down potential customers. Get those lists, sort them according to your unique criteria, and add the results to your master list. Make sure to code them as speculative contacts, though, to distinguish them from existing customers. And once these potential buyers become actual customers, make sure to update their entries with appropriate buyer codes. Eventually, you will be able to track which speculative customers cross over to the *actual* customer category and learn how well your spec lists are working. Spec names that don't produce within a reasonable time should be removed.

For other lists, look to potential selling partners in your area. Make a list of every group sales database that exists or is likely to exist in your market and take some time to think about which ones would benefit you most. Once you know which lists are worth going after, decide what you would be willing to offer to gain access to those databases. Your list may be a valuable bargaining tool to leverage access to additional names. Start by offering a name-for-name trade. Otherwise, think about in-kind goods or services or even cash if the list has exceptional value.

Group lists are extremely valuable and any proprietary list should be vigorously protected. Naturally you wouldn't want to give your list to anyone. Always trade on a name-for-name basis with a one-time only usage agreement and always use an independent third party mail house for joint mailings so that nobody has access to your data. If you have top repeat buyers that you'd rather not share, take them off the list before trading.

CUSTOMER RELATIONSHIP MANAGEMENT

Customer relationship management or CRM refers to the methods businesses use to keep their customers and make sure they continue to buy. The best customer relationship management technique is direct, personal customer contact. Businesses that have large lists of customers, however, need techniques for communicating with them in efficient but not necessarily personal ways.

In group sales, CRM refers to the personal interaction you'll maintain with your top-producing customers, the effective communications and quality personal service you'll offer to your periodic customers, and the incentives, offers, or rewards you'll make available to your entire universe of buyers. No matter what your CRM methods are you cannot hope to maintain relationships with your customers if you don't know who they are, what they need, what their patronage has meant to you, and how you can reach them with meaningful communications.

Your database is your most valuable CRM tool but it has to be sharpened on a regular basis to keep it effective. Undifferentiated group sales databases are inefficient and obsolete. Carefully coded databases, on the other hand, are powerful marketing machines that can refine your group sales outreach with scientific precision.

Subscribers and Customer Relationship Management:

When it comes to subscribers, the stage entertainment industry has nearly perfected customer relationship management. Regional subscription organizations offer their subscribers extraordinary services and incentives to earn their continued patronage. But group buyers—even though individual group buyers represent more ticket revenue than individual subscribers—are lucky to get a generic brochure every now and then.

Suppose one of your charter subscribers has held a pair of tickets since the mid 1970s and the average value of those seats has been roughly four hundred and fifty dollars per year for a total of thirteen thousand dollars across the life of the subscription. How do the perks available to that subscriber compare to the perks your organization makes available to group buyers who spend thirteen thousand dollars in one season? How about group buyers who spend thirteen thousand dollars *every* season?

Group sellers might do well to craft meaningful CRM programs that do for group buyers what subscription programs do for subscribers. For an even better example of effective CRM, look at the donor recognition programs in not-for-profit development departments.

Do you have a plan for managing relationships with your top customers?

Sell

Now that you've made your plan, done your homework and gotten your data squared away, it is time to go out into the world and *sell* tickets.

Start by reorganizing your group sales office so there is someone to handle operations and customer service and someone to seek out and sell to new buyers. You'll never be able to make new sales happen if you are sitting at your desk answering the phone or shuffling paperwork. Of course staffing will be a huge issue but let's assume for the sake of this chapter that you have found a solution that frees you from the day-to-day burden of reactive sales activity.

Here are some specific recommendations for outbound sales that should keep a proactive salesperson busy and productive for a full year:

Identify the customers who bought the most tickets or spent the most money over the last three years. Call them and arrange to meet with them. Go to their offices if possible or invite them to lunch. Bring them gifts and some new inside information about your shows. Ask them to tell you honestly how things have been going and listen very carefully to what they tell you. Ask them what you can do to make it easier for them to buy more tickets and promise them you'll explore the feasibility of doing what they ask. Ask them to show you their offices and introduce you to their staff, if appropriate. Let them teach you as much as they like about their businesses and how your tickets fit in to what they do. Do everything you can to establish a warm, personal, accommodating relationship with these customers and learn everything you can about their needs and expectations. When you get back to your office, follow up with appropriate thank-you notes and do everything you promised.

Identify your top twenty-five *prospective* customers. Call them and ask to meet with them. Bring them gifts and clear, specific, relevant, customer-oriented information about your products. Tell them why you have selected them and why you believe it is in their interest to buy tickets from you. Listen to what they tell you about their needs and expectations. If you sense there is a fit, explore ways to work together. When you get back to your office, send appropriate thank-you notes, do what you promised you'd do, and follow through with the ones you feel offer the most potential.

Identify your top twenty-five community partners—all the destination management companies, hotel sales executives, restaurants, caterers, event venues, theme parks, attractions, charter companies, sightseeing companies, and destination marketing organizations, for example. Call each one and ask for a meeting with the person who oversees sales to group buyers. Tell them what you do and ask if they'd like to explore the possibility of working together. Tell them how your product augments their product then discuss the feasibility of co-promotions. Offer to cross sell or make referrals, then ask for cross selling and referrals in exchange. When you get back, do your follow-up and move forward on the partnerships that show the most promise.

Identify the destination marketing organizations and trade associations you should be working with. Join them and participate meaningfully in their activities. Go to all meetings, conventions, and events that fit with your objectives and budget and make a point of networking with potential customers, partners, and referral sources. Be a part of the industries you are courting. Professional group buyers want to do business with people who are part of their world.

Keep all the people you meet on a VIP list and make sure to invite them to your shows whenever possible. A good group sales office will have a list ready every time the venue needs to paper.

Always paper with people who influence future sales, and don't just invite them to the unpopular shows that need help. Be on hand to greet your friends and clients when they come to the show and make a point of knowing them by name. Relationships are the key to group sales and your ability to create positive, productive relationships with your clientele will go a long way toward increasing and sustaining sales.

These recommendations call for two or three out-of-office sales meetings per week plus a variety of receptions, meetings, trade shows, and marketplaces. With the necessary follow-up it is easily a full-time job that requires more than fifty percent out-of-office activity. Assuming the product you are selling is desirable, if you target your prospects carefully, establish quality relationships, and sell persuasively, you will more than cover the cost of hiring the necessary in-office administrative support.

If you find yourself getting bogged down in reactive customer service and not being able to keep up with the productive outbound sales work, don't let yourself get sucked back into the rut. Work with your organization's leadership on a sensible plan to enable you to maintain a proactive sales effort.

Keep at it for two years or more to assess adequately its effectiveness. It might take three years for some of your new target markets to begin showing real results so don't give up too soon.

Make that call:

Picking up the phone to make sales calls can be daunting. Here are five tips for making the call as effective as possible.

DO YOUR HOMEWORK

If you are going to call someone, learn everything you can about their organization and the work they do first. "I noticed on your website you were doing a promotion with…"

WRITE A SCRIPT

Write out exactly what you plan to say when your contact answers the phone and have three questions ready to ask if the conversation isn't moving.

KNOW EXACTLY WHAT YOU WANT AND ASK FOR IT

If you want one hour of that person's time to learn what they know, ask for it in straightforward language. "I'd like to spend an hour with you to ask you questions about group sales. It would be my pleasure to invite you to a show or take you to lunch in exchange for the opportunity."

STAY FOCUSED ON WHAT'S IN IT FOR THEM

If it is a win-win promotion, stay focused on what they win. If you are asking for something that doesn't offer a win for them, buy them lunch or offer them free tickets. It may be about you, but as far as they're concerned, it's about them.

BE FRIENDLY, PERSONABLE, AND SINCERE

People do business with people they like, people they feel comfortable with, and people they trust.

Calling people you don't know can become second nature if you plan and make a habit of doing it regularly. Ultimately, sales is about talking to people, so pick up that phone!

Market

Your strategic plan should include a marketing component designed to promote the shows you sell and the wonderful services you offer to volume ticket buyers. In general, there are two ways to market group sales: piggybacking on existing show marketing that is aimed at individual consumers and developing an independent marketing effort aimed exclusively at group buyers.

PIGGYBACKING

Selling group tickets is not always the marketing department's top priority so your strategic group sales marketing plan may need to remind your colleagues why, when and how group sales should be included in their single-ticket marketing programs. Remember, group revenue can represent anywhere from five to twenty-five percent or more of total sales so the group message deserves a reasonable share of the space or time allotted to the consumer marketing message.

Start by working with your GM and senior marketing staffer on a document that outlines exactly how the group sales message will be integrated into the single-ticket marketing plan. If you get buy-in from your colleagues up front, you'll create an objective reference that will prevent arbitrary decision-making, such as dropping the group number from the ad or forgetting to put the group message in the brochure. Here are some general guidelines for creating a win-win agreement between group sales and the marketing department:

- Decide what overall percentage of space will be allocated to the group message, how those percentages are managed in each medium and what circumstances will influence changes in the allocations.

- Determine in advance which ads will carry the group sales message. Is it in every print ad larger than six column inches? Every sixty-second radio ad? Anything on TV?

- Decide on a specific approach to online group sales and agree how groups will be integrated into the organization's website. Remember, your website is, first and foremost, a sales tool so group sales needs to be front and center.

- Determine exactly how the group message will appear in print ads or collateral. Make sure the message is persuasive and that you don't waste an opportunity to tip a smaller group into the official group category: "Book 15 or more and save! Call 800-555-9090 or visit www.showgrouptix.com." If you need three different size messages for different types of ads or collateral, write them out and make them part of the agreement.

- Map out how the group message will appear in direct marketing messages and what percentage of available space will be dedicated to them.

- Consider creating a brand for group sales with an exclusive logo or tagline that reinforces the group message with cumulative exposure, i.e., "Groups get More!" Write up a brief brand management document that becomes part of the marketing agreement so everyone knows when and how to use the group sales brand.

Determine in advance how marketing and group sales interrelate, and put it in writing so that it is well understood.

Single-ticket marketing is your most cost-effective resource for sending the group message because it is usually covered by another budget and it reaches the broadest possible consumer market. You'll want to get as much out of it as you can.

INDEPENDENT GROUP MARKETING

You also have many options for sending the group sales message on its own through consumer media, targeted group media, and direct marketing channels. Make sure your strategic plan includes a group sales marketing component that outlines the methods to be used. Make sure it covers:

- Direct mail marketing to in-house lists, acquired databases, partner databases, speculative lists, trade association membership databases, etc.

- Direct email marketing to in-house lists, acquired databases, partner databases, speculative lists, trade association membership databases, etc.

- Print advertising in local consumer publications, such as business journals, senior newspapers, religious newspapers, community newspapers, and affinity organization newsletters

- Print advertising in targeted group media such as *Group Tour Magazine, Group Travel Leader*, CVB publications, and magazines associated with the trade organizations to which you belong

- Above-the-line media advertising—big shows in large markets have found limited success with above-the-line group advertising on radio or with print ads targeted to groups

- Special advertising, promotions, and collateral distribution for networking meetings, conventions, trade events, or marketplaces

- Targeted letter/collateral campaigns for new speculative markets, such as fundraising executives or affinity groups

- Cooperative promotions and collateral distribution with destination partners and travel companies

- Online marketing of web-based group booking services

Such a list is limited only by your creativity and the extent of your budget resources. Map out your marketing strategy, project your returns, monitor your successes, and continue to refine your group sales marketing program.

Selling Groups
on the Web:

The web is your most important sales mechanism. Right now the phone is probably handling most of your business but the web will eclipse it soon, and there is no excuse for not being ahead of the trend.

If you haven't done it yet, plan to launch new group sales booking pages in the next three months. You may not be able to offer direct online booking out of live inventory but you can do a lot to stimulate sales and streamline services.

Here are a few things that should be on your group sales web pages:

ORGANIZATION HOME PAGE: The purpose of the website is to sell tickets so the group sales button should be positioned prominently on your organization's home page. If possible, it should carry a persuasive message that entices visitors to click: "Group Savings," "Groups Get More," "Book 15 and Save!," "Click here for Group Specials," etc.

GROUP SALES HOME PAGE: On this page explain group sales in clear, concise, persuasive language and offer easy-to-follow navigation tools for accessing the rest of the group pages. Copy should be geared to newcomers and veterans alike. Stress your most compelling reasons why group booking is a good idea.

HOW TO BOOK A GROUP: This can be a part of your group sales home page or a page all its own. Explain how simple it is to go through the ordering process. Provide convenient click-to navigation buttons for group pricing and seating maps. Make it sound easy, convenient, and worthwhile. Provide suggestions to trigger the thinking you want the customer to do: "A fresh and fun way to celebrate special occasions."

ONLINE BOOKING: On this page, walk customers through the booking process. If they can book directly out of live inventory, make sure the process is clean and straightforward. If they need to place a request that will be confirmed later, make sure they can submit all the necessary information in a simple form that gets emailed to you. Tell them exactly what will happen when they submit a request and always respond in the manner you've promised: "You will be contacted by a group sales representative in one business day."

PRINTABLE ORDER FORM: Make sure you post an order form that online customers can download and mail or fax to you. Some people won't want to submit a request online.

GROUP PARTIES, DINING, ENTERTAINMENT: Use this page to let group buyers know how they can make events out of their group visit or how they can add valuable package components to their group itineraries. Promote your local partners prominently and link to them whenever possible.

SPECIALS, PACKAGES, AND MORE: Use this page to describe all the great promotional offers you've got with local partners. This is also a great place to list other local attractions and services, to boast about what a wonderful group destination your area is, and to mention what other wonderful things your customers can do nearby.

IMPORTANT: Include your phone, fax, and email contact information on every page. Many websites try to steer customers away from traditional phone services. You, on the other hand, are trying to get more sales and improve your services, so make sure your customers feel free to pick up the phone and call.

Other things to include:

GROUP SALES POLICIES AND PROCEDURES: Write these in a concise format and post them where they'll help customers understand what to expect in terms of confirmations, deadlines, and restrictions. If your restrictions and disclaimers sound harsh, punitive, or legalistic, rewrite them in the friendliest possible language. If you can't do that, bury them or don't post them on the web. You can always make sure they are printed in small type on the back of your invoices.

ACCESS INFORMATION: Tell groups how to get to the venue, where the buses can pull up, where buses can park, and add any other logistical details to help group planners organize their trip. If you are going to make them click to a page that discusses access for single-ticket buyers, make sure it has information that is relevant to groups as well.

SCHEDULE, PRICING AND SEATING MAPS: If you are selling groups on an advance priority basis, post the dates and special prices in the groups section where single-ticket-buying consumers won't see them. Otherwise, have them click to a generic price and schedule page that includes group information.

SPECIAL SERVICE FOR DIFFERENT BUYER TYPES: If you have different services for different types of buyers, send them to special pages: Travel Professionals, Meeting and Event Planners, Volume Buyers Club, etc.

PRIVATE ACCESS PAGES: If you offer special deals to certain types of buyers, or if you have promotions with limited distribution, give these customers a password and post the insider deals on a members-only page that can be accessed by typing in a code.

WANT MORE HELP? Search the web for venues that are similar to yours and find out what your colleagues in other destinations are doing. You'll see a few folks doing great things, and you'll see a lot of folks doing little more than posting passive online group sales brochures. Take your cue from the web-savvy sellers who are pushing the envelope.

BUT WAIT, THERE'S MORE! Don't launch group web booking pages and then forget them. You've got to market this service heavily and train your customers to use it. The more booking you can move online, the more time you'll have to devote to outbound sales.

Promote your online group booking services and web address wherever you promote your phone number. Link to your groups home page wherever possible—especially through your strategic selling partners and trade relationships. And always look for creative ways to drive more business through your website.

Compete

When it comes to group dollars, you are competing with every attraction, destination, or activity a group can buy. These can include but are not limited to:

- Casinos and gaming destinations

- Shopping complexes

- National parks and historic sites

- Theme parks

- Museums, zoos, and cultural attractions

- Theme restaurants

- Legit theatres and road houses

- Educational destinations of all kinds

- Regional, seasonal, or specialized sightseeing (leaf peeping, birding, whale watching)

- Remote entertainment destinations that are perceived to be superior (Broadway, Toronto, Las Vegas)

- Cruises of all lengths and sizes

- Resorts of every description

- Entertainment destinations such as Branson or Myrtle Beach

- Luxury corporate events with privately booked or produced entertainment

- Sporting events

- Arena entertainment, such as ice shows and circuses

- Dinner theatres and themed dinner/entertainment complexes, such as Medieval Times or Arabian Nights

- Other stage entertainment including most local legit theatres and their low-cost alternatives

- Fairs, festivals, and special events

- Face-to-face group activities such as picnics, bowling, dances, reunions, and family get-togethers.

Group sales professionals representing all the organizations on this list are fighting hard to get group buyers' attention. Your job as a group salesperson is to understand exactly where your product fits in to this competitive arena and position it accordingly. Professional stage entertainment may be one of the more appealing options available to group buyers, but failing to compete can render even the most attractive products invisible.

Here are several ways to learn about the companies competing against you:

Examine your CVB membership list and identify every company that is seeking group business. Separate them into three categories: competitors, potential package partners and customers (yes, you will probably find some of your customers on these lists among the DMCs, hotels, or local tour operators). Keep your customers happy, forge alliances with your strategic partners, and work hard to provide better products and services than your competitors. Also, find out how your competitors are selling: never let them own a target market that you haven't bothered to approach.

Visit your day-trip tour operator customers and ask to see all their other tour packages in your region. Don't be surprised if they show you a catalog containing dozens of tours in addition to the ones that include your show. Ask them to describe how the tours that include your shows stack up against all the other offerings. Then ask what you can do to make them more marketable or more profitable to the operator.

Convene a focus group of select group clients and ask them to tell you what goes into their decision-making process. Ask them to describe the choices that are available to them, and ask them what factors cause them to lean in one direction or another.

Visit your local DMCs and ask them to describe all the ideas they typically present to a client who is planning a group visit to your area. If they don't automatically mention your venue or shows, ask them what you can do to make your products more appealing or user friendly for DMCs and their clients.

Join MPI, NTA, ABA, or any other relevant trade organization and meet the thousands of group sales professionals who buy and sell group products. Meet group sales professionals who represent stage entertainment products in other markets and ask them how they deal with their competition. Meet prospective group clients and ask them to honestly appraise how your product stacks up against the other products that are available to them.

Call your local DMO anonymously and ask them what sort of leisure activity they'd recommend for a visiting group. If they don't recommend your shows, get closer to them and make sure you are mentioned when they are asked to make recommendations.

All this competition can be daunting, but entering the competitive arena can also introduce you to more customers, more ideas for reaching out to new customers, and more opportunities for partnering with non-competitive group attractions and service providers. Moreover, your active participation in trade associations and marketplaces makes you top-of-mind when your friends, colleagues, and destination marketing organizations are called upon to make referrals.

Knowing your competition also forces you to sharpen your persuasive arguments, refine your service standards, and meet your customers' needs in the most efficient manner. Group salespeople who compete become better group salespeople and that means more tickets, more revenue, and more growth for you as a sales professional.

The choice is yours: sit in your office and take what comes or get out there and fight for your fair share of the available group sales business. If you are a *sales* professional, there is only one option.

What happens
at these trade shows?

Trade association gatherings can be excellent places to do business with prospective customers. At the annual National Tour Association convention, for example, four hundred and fifty or so North American tour operators gather to meet with the thousands of suppliers who sell them their hotels, attractions, entertainment, meals, and other travel services.

The convention is centered around a series of seven-minute meetings that take place over three days. These meetings are computer scheduled and based on requests that are submitted in advance by both suppliers and buyers. During the appointment sessions, operators are stationed in booths on the trade show floor and suppliers walk—or run—from one pre-scheduled meeting to the next and give seven-minute sales pitches or negotiate new business with old customers. In some cases, suppliers meet with forty or more buyers in one day!

Surrounding the business sessions are six days of educational programs and networking events that enable buyers to learn more about the package travel industry and establish personal as well as professional relationships with their NTA customers.

Not all trade events follow this format, and not all trade associations are right for all suppliers, but if your principal competitors or community partners are meeting NTA tour operators every year at the national convention, you might want to be there, too!

Serve

In an intensely competitive market, it is essential that the customer service you offer be as good as, if not better than, that of your competition. This may be difficult in an industry that puts such a low priority on group sales, so the responsibility is on you, the group seller, to make sure your service standards and those of your company meet or exceed your customers' expectations.

Start by examining the competition for those group entertainment dollars and study the companies that offer the best service. Is Disney on the list? Is Hard Rock Café? Is the zoo or the Hall of Fame or the river cruise or Imax or the casino? Or how about the dinner theatre out in the suburbs that always has so many buses in the parking lot?

Ask yourself what the service is like at the top competitors then ask yourself how it compares with the service group customers get from you. Better yet, ask your customers to compare your service with the service they get from everyone else. Be prepared. What they tell you might not be flattering. No matter how nice you and your group sales staff are, the stage entertainment industry can make good group service operationally difficult and it can put us in an awkward position relative to our competitors.

Here is a checklist of minimum service standards that every professional group sales office should uphold. Compare this with the service you offer now. If you are not meeting the minimum standards, see which improvements you can make right away and then work with your management team to plan for achieving all of them in the near future.

- All forms of public information contain clear, accurate, detailed, persuasive, user-friendly, customer-oriented group sales messages.

- Group sales materials are professionally produced and their messages recognize and reflect the needs and expectations of multiple target markets representing both consumers and businesses. No more generic ads and brochures that are merely warmed over single-ticket pieces.

- Group on-sale dates and performance schedules are created with group clientele in mind so that B-to-B group buyers have maximum lead time, earliest possible information, and access to the broadest spectrum of available performances—even if those performances are not yet on sale to the local consumer public. PR and marketing won't like this, but the downside is negligible and the upside, if you work it right, is well worth any miscommunication with your single-ticket markets.

- Group buyers receive rewards for their advance volume purchases in the form of first-come, first-served seating (in good seating locations), flexible terms, discounts, perks, priority service, etc. The more tickets a buyer purchases, the greater his or her rewards.

- Easy-to-find online resources contain complete, accurate, up-to-date information and provide convenient methods for placing online group ticket orders, or at the very least, requests by email or faxable, downloadable order forms. If you can sell direct from inventory, do it!

- Office hours are consistent and phones are answered promptly by human beings during published hours of operation. No exceptions. In a business where any call can represent thousands of dollars in sales, there is no excuse for not answering phones. None. No, don't even think about it.

- Customer service reps are friendly, accommodating, deferential group sales professionals, not entry-level entertainment industry wannabes. All staffers are completely customer oriented and fully trained on the needs and expectations of the various clients they are expected to service.

- All policies and procedures are set according to what will serve the customers best and sell the most tickets, not based on outdated operational traditions, irrational biases, or that's-the-way-we've-always-done-it attitudes.

- Orders are confirmed instantly or, if remote box office confirmation is required, within hours. No order should ever go unconfirmed for more than one business day.

- Payment terms allow maximum flexibility to the customer (not maximum convenience for the venue's operations staff) but stop short of placing the venue or show at risk.

- Tickets are delivered promptly with packets that contain useful materials such as ticket-holder rosters, restaurant guides, bus parking details, order forms for upcoming shows, order forms for bulk merchandise, and study guides.

- All customers get white-glove treatment but top-producing customers and repeat buyers get premium personal service. In not-for-profit organizations, top volume buyers should get tiered perks modeled after donor recognition programs.

- Groups get red-carpet treatment on site from house staff and/or group sales staff if possible. Some venues offer step-on meet and greet service: a representative of the show welcomes guests before they get off the coach. In some markets, like Branson, Missouri, the stars of the shows have been known to step on the bus, pick up the mike, and welcome the crowd to their performance!

- Group buyer names are entered onto a well-organized database with details about buyer type and sales history. All database names are used according to a coordinated customer relationship management program.

- Group buyers receive regular communications from the group sales department that are targeted by buyer type, relevant to individual needs and expectations, and sent through the most appropriate medium, such as email, mail, outbound phones, special delivery of client gifts, or in-person interaction.

- Group buyers are never insulted, punished, or otherwise disincentivized by poorly coordinated marketing programs, miscommunications, or promotional offers that undercut their ability to assemble groups, resell tickets, or work productively with you or your organization.

Upgrading your service standards is the least expensive, most effective way to increase ticket sales. If you can't achieve all of these right away, do what you can and work hard to make the rest happen as soon as possible.

Partner

It has been said several times in this book that the best way to find new markets is to team up with partners in your community who have already developed their group clientele and are willing to participate in win-win cooperative promotions. Partnering enables you to expand your reach and enhance your product's appeal by adding attractive package components, by highlighting the value of the destination experience, or by capitalizing on your destination's pre-existing group customer base.

Create a list of all the businesses and organizations in your area that court groups. Select the ones who are not direct competitors and jot down a few ideas for creating mutually beneficial partnership programs. Should you and the group sales manager from the hotel next door be attending ABA together? Should you and the sales director from Ye Olde Spaghetti Plantation be promoting a special dinner/theatre package? Does the local historic sightseeing company have a fabulous list of student group buyers from outside the area? Should that big motor coach charter company be sending your SMERF mailer to their list of charter customers? How about that high-end restaurant ownership group or the convention center or the botanical garden or the battlefield museum or the elder hostel or the university summer housing department?

After you've prioritized your list, visit your potential partners to toss around ideas. It is a great way to meet other professionals in the industry and you're bound to come up with a few motivated colleagues. If you are lucky, you'll find partners who value the opportunity so much they'll be willing to sell your group tickets just to enhance the value of their own product!

Go to your DMOs and work with them on cooperative strategies. Ask them to recommend potential partners and make sure they keep you informed about cooperative sales and marketing opportunities. Volunteer! Serve on committees, attend events, take key staff to lunch, and go to all networking functions. Hey, why not host the next networking event? The closer you are to your destination marketing organization, the closer you will be to your most promising partners and the visitor markets you and your partners need to tap.

Share the wealth! The concept of zealously guarding databases and circling the wagons to protect turf is hopelessly out of date. Your group mailing list is a hot commodity that you can use to garner valuable cooperative promotional opportunities. Use the equity you've built in your database to leverage access to data resources you don't have. Give what you can—without giving away the store—and know that expanding the market for everyone is the best way to expand the market for your organization.

Ultimately, group sellers who engage in the most proactive, dynamic win-win partnerships are the ones who will expand their reach, open new markets, generate incremental growth, and lay a foundation for future expansion. They are also the ones who will have the most fun, meet the most people, achieve the most professional growth, and network toward greater career opportunities!

Change

At the beginning of this book we spoke of entertainment industry traditions that date back to Elizabethan times—traditions that still influence how we produce and promote our products. Group sales traditions are somewhat younger but they still date back fifty years to the middle of the twentieth century—a very different time when local, communal group activity was a fundamental aspect of North American society.

Times have changed and if we want to keep our venues full, we're going to have to change, too. The fact is that most of the methods and traditions that govern group sales were created for another time in a very different world. If we expect to tap new markets and deliver new group buyers in greater numbers, we will have to change the way we do business. We will have to question the very foundations of some decades-old assumptions and ask hard questions about their legitimacy. We will have to examine how we do business and determine if our methods are appropriate for the world we live in today.

But introducing change in a change-averse industry isn't easy. If you want to introduce change in your organization, you'll have to manage the process with skill and finesse. Here are some practical suggestions for managing change and making it more palatable to your colleagues.

Learn all you can about why things work the way they do and separate what is traditional from what is required by contract. It is much easier to change operational habit than it is to change legal agreements with box office unions, venue owners, touring companies, ticketing concerns, producers, and presenters, for example.

Identify the changes that you believe will facilitate increased sales and assign them a priority: Must be Made, Should be Made, Next Year, Three Year Plan, Back Burner. Consider the political landscape, weigh the pros and cons of making your suggestions, then reprioritize your list based on what battles you believe can be won with minimal losses.

Support any recommendation with an airtight case. Provide testimony from professionals with whom you have consulted. Provide examples of how the changes you recommend have been successful elsewhere. Provide letters from potential customers explaining what they need and how giving them what they want will enable them to buy more tickets. Create clear, concise, supportable financial projections that identify in tickets and dollars exactly why the changes you are recommending are profitable. Always point to objective facts and keep the level of discourse focused on ultimate priorities, such as new audiences and incremental revenue.

Anticipate objections from all quarters and remember that selling tickets and earning revenue don't top everyone's priority list. Consider artistic ego, turf battles, administrative workload, irrational bias against groups, funding priorities, resistance to commercialism, and professional jealousies. Ultimately, selling more tickets helps everyone but various colleagues will need to be shown exactly what's in it for them and why they don't have to feel threatened.

Communicate personally, clearly, persuasively, and non-confrontationally with all parties who have an interest in the decision. Start with your direct supervisor then go to the most influential opinion leaders—board members, executive producers, CEOs, GMs, etc.—and work your way through the organization from there. Keep everyone in the loop and keep everyone aware of why it will be in their best interest to support the changes you recommend.

Bring the policy makers face to face with the customers. If your executive leaders and operational staff don't have personal relationships with the people who buy the most tickets, make sure they meet them, thank them for their business, and listen to their concerns. Set up meetings and let your bosses know that they will be meeting their largest customers—individuals who buy thousands of dollars worth of tickets.

Gently educate the rest of your organization to help overcome the myths that stand in the way of increased volume sales. Hand them this book when you're through and ask them to read Part 1.

Sit back, relax, take a deep breath, stay focused on the big picture, and accept all things with grace and equanimity. It is a long, slow process but opening new markets to bring more volume ticket buyers into our shows is one of the most important jobs that a theatre, performing arts, or stage entertainment professional can do.

Change won't be easy but any change that involves selling more tickets is good for the industry and worth the time and energy it takes to make it happen.

Business Email:

Email is a great way to communicate with your colleagues about issues on which people agree but it is not a good way to bring about change. If you want to change the way people think in your organization, do as much face-to-face communicating as possible. If you are working on potentially contentious issues, make sure the parties who disagree are encouraged to speak together in the presence of a senior decision maker. Get your colleagues to agree in person, then go back to your office and back it up with emails that repeat and confirm what you've discussed.

Email is an extraordinary communication tool but it can never replace human interaction.

Innovate

Here's a short history of stage entertainment marketing.

We begin in the early twentieth century with publicists. For several decades shows used publicists to pitch news stories, place print ads, and make sure the three-sheets and window cards got up in the right places. In the old days, entertainment promotions were pretty much local affairs that played out on the pages of influential daily newspapers and on theatre marquees.

Eventually, sprawling populations and expanding electronic media opportunities meant more places to pitch stories and new places to advertise. As advertising grew in importance, press reps began handing off some of the responsibility to advertising agencies. So for much of the 1970s and 1980s, press reps and ad agencies shared the responsibility for "publicizing" stage shows and getting the word out to local markets about the shows that were available to them.

Profound changes in the 1980s saw regional not-for-profits, institutional presenters, and corporate producers working on a more strategic approach. This sensibility was based on the idea that communicating with the world about the shows was a coordinated strategic function called marketing. By the end of the twentieth century, successful shows were likely to be the product of integrated marketing campaigns that determined how publicity, advertising, promotions, direct marketing, and grass-roots initiatives worked together for maximum impact.

But throughout the 1990s, amidst the high visibility clamor of marketing, advertising, and publicity, a quieter movement was gaining strength. Little by little, sales rose from the realm of afterthought to a position of begrudging acceptance and perhaps even limited respect. By the beginning of the new century, sales had demonstrated a potency that few marketers, advertisers, or publicists had expected, and it pointed in directions that offered interesting possibilities.

Today, sales is poised to become the next major trend in entertainment ticketing. Borrowing from more business-oriented methods in the consumer products and services industries, sales is expanding on traditional methods by adding a necessary persuasive component. Sales has taken what had been a passive process of *informing* customers and turned it into a proactive one that involves *urging* customers to buy tickets. Proactive sales initiatives identify and approach new customers with persuasive sales pitches that say, "This is all about YOU! How many tickets would YOU like us to make available for YOU today?" Until the 1990s few people had bothered to look for promising new markets, let alone stand face to face with volume ticket buyers and describe what's in it for them while offering to make it easy for them to obtain the tickets they need.

What proactive sales pioneers have discovered is a world of untapped business-to-business volume ticket potential that the publicists, ad agencies, and marketers hadn't known. Today the stage entertainment industry sits astride a line that may lead to an era where producers not only publicize, advertise and market their products, but where they actually go out and sell them, too.

Group sales has been at the forefront of profound changes in the stage entertainment industry in the last fifteen years—changes that will determine how this industry does business in the future. Group sales is where business-to-business practices, FIT contract sales, packaging, sales partnerships, online travel wholesaling, tourism industry promotions, destination marketing, and cultural tourism all gained a foothold. Many of these have already become hot industry trends while B-to-B partnerships, wholesaling, and online packaging stand to become powerful new generators of ticket purchases on both the groups and single-ticket sides of the industry.

Because you are a proactive, outbound seller of volume tickets to both consumer and B-to-B buyers, you will be exposed to more outside business influences than anyone else in your organization. You will be in a position to learn how other businesses sell bulk products, such as tickets, travel, room nights, admissions, and meals. You'll see that these products are all the same: the right to occupy a certain space for a certain length of time. It doesn't matter if it's a theatre seat, a hotel room, a seat on a plane, a chair in a restaurant, or a chance to pass through the gates at Six-Flags. From the perspective of the business model, we are all selling similar products and some of us are doing it with far more sophistication and far more success than others.

You, dear sales professional, must learn which methods work in other businesses and which ones will also work in ours. You must become the prophet who visits the other side, sees the light of truth, and returns to show your mortal colleagues the way. Then you must find ways to introduce new methods of doing business in an industry that is complacent, egotistical, and stubbornly resistant to change. You must see the potential for yourself and find ways to share that vision with people who are afraid or unwilling to open their eyes.

This is the moment for innovation. This is the moment for growth. This is the moment for business. This is the moment when our industry will be asked to recognize that change is imminent and unavoidable. This is the moment that defines the future—the moment that heralds a new era. This is the dawn of the "era of sales" and you, my dear group sales professional, are holding the torch.

What you do with it is up to you.

Group Methods Overview

Embrace these methods and you will sell more tickets, earn more revenue, expand your professional horizons, learn more, travel more, meet more people, advance your career, have more fun, and contribute to profound changes in the live entertainment industry. What have you got to lose?

CREATE A STRATEGIC PLAN

A good strategic plan will make your job easy because you'll always know where you are and what you need to do.

LEARN FROM YOUR COLLEAGUES AND PEERS

Interacting with talented professionals in your market helps you sell more, gives you opportunities to package, and helps to increase the overall market for your destination.

ORGANIZE AND USE YOUR DATA

If your mailing list is a mysterious mess, you need to learn who's on it and what kind of buyers they are before you can go after new targets. Your database is your foundation. You need to make sure it is sound before starting any new construction.

SELL YOUR PRODUCTS

If you are not out selling your product, you might as well change your name from group sales to group operations. Get out and find new buyers then create ways to serve them.

MARKET YOUR PRODUCTS

Hey, if the folks over in marketing are already spending money, get your message in there. And don't pass up useful opportunities to target market your products and services independently.

COMPETE WITH YOUR COMPETITION

If your group customers have money, there are a lot of people who want it. You have to know who your competitors are and what they're doing in order to compete effectively. Then you have to be present and visible in their competitive arenas.

GIVE EXCELLENT CUSTOMER SERVICE

The products we sell can't be beat, but the service we provide is surpassed by just about everyone. Find the best service provider in your market and strive to surpass them. If your operational infrastructure makes that difficult, change the way your organization does business.

PARTNER FOR PACKAGES

Group events are package events. If all you are doing is selling tickets, you are missing excellent opportunities to meet your customers' needs in fresh, creative, effective ways.

IF IT ISN'T WORKING, <u>CHANGE</u> IT.

Nobody wants to change—especially if he or she thinks everything's been going along just fine for the last six hundred years. But you're going to have to manage change if you expect to open and serve new markets.

USHER IN A NEW ERA

Some group salespeople are sitting in basements taking calls from group leaders and processing paperwork. Others are making profound changes in the way the stage entertainment industry taps and serves new volume ticket markets. You?

Authors' Biographies

TREVOR O'DONNELL is a nationally recognized marketing and sales consultant who specializes in stage entertainment and entertainment-related travel destinations. In the past twenty years Trevor has promoted numerous forms of live entertainment and performing arts on Broadway, in London's West End, and in cities across North America including Los Angeles, Las Vegas, and San Francisco.

In New York Trevor developed innovative sales and marketing initiatives for Theatre Direct International (TDI), a theatrical sales and marketing agency created by producer Cameron Mackintosh (*Cats, The Phantom of the Opera, Les Misérables, Miss Saigon*, etc.) to market Broadway and London theatre to regional consumers and the domestic and international tourism industries. Together with veteran Broadway marketers Bob Hoffman and Bruce Amick, he developed and managed a groundbreaking destination-marketing cooperative that carried the Broadway message to tourism markets worldwide.

In Los Angeles Trevor directed marketing efforts for Disney's long-running hometown production of *The Lion King* at the Pantages Theatre in Hollywood. Before joining Disney, Trevor created record-breaking sales initiatives for Center Theatre Group's Ahmanson Theatre and the Mark Taper Forum. He has also worked with the Music Center of Los Angeles to launch new destination-marketing campaigns and marketing strategies for "Dance at the Music Center."

One of the nation's foremost experts in theatrical group sales, Trevor has opened and tapped new business-to-business markets for Broadway, for touring productions of Broadway shows, and for regional presenting theatres in American destination cities large and small. His recent work has included B-to-B sales development for top entertainment companies including Cirque du Soleil, *The Producers*, and Blue Man Productions' *Blue Man Group* in Las Vegas.

Trevor has extensive experience in all aspects of marketing, sales, and development for not-for-profit arts organizations. He has worked for a variety of producers, presenters, and arts centers including Manhattan Theatre Club, Symphony Space, Newark

Symphony Hall, the New Brunswick Cultural Center, The Mattress Factory, Pittsburgh Public Theatre, and Pittsburgh Symphony Orchestra.

Trevor is also an educator who has taught communications courses at noted colleges, universities, and professional education centers. He holds an MA in Communications from Bowling Green State University and a BS in Speech, Theatre, and Music from Emerson College in Boston.

BOB HOFMANN is a recognized leader in live entertainment sales & marketing, and one of the nation's foremost marketers of stage entertainment to the world travel industry. He has nineteen years of experience in management and marketing, twelve of which he spent as vice-president of sales and marketing for Theatre Direct International/Broadway.com (TDI), where he helped to build a small in-house group sales operation into one of New York's top theatrical sales and marketing agencies. During his time at TDI, Bob opened and developed new domestic and international markets, generating many millions of dollars in revenue for stage entertainment in New York and London.

Bob is currently a partner and president of Broadway Inbound, a marketing company that connects producers of stage entertainment with worldwide business and consumer markets through the domestic and international tourism industries. Bob has served on the board of directors of NYC & Co. (New York City's Convention & Visitors Bureau), on the board of the Receptive Services Association, and on the board and executive committee of The National Tour Association.

As assistant producing director for the Pittsburgh Public Theatre, Bob participated in producing over eighteen plays and in the day-to-day operations of a $3.5 million arts organization and facility. He worked as casting director with Joseph Abaldo Casting, was co-founder and artistic director of United Stage, and worked as production stage manager for the Bathhouse Theatre in Seattle, Washington.

Bob has extensive experience with commercial, educational, and not-for-profit performing arts organizations and has worked in both management and production in numerous capacities. He has been associated with The Great Performers at Lincoln Center, The New York City Ballet, The Seattle Symphony, The New City Theatre of Seattle, The City Theatre of Pittsburgh, The Carnegie Mellon Repertory Theatre, Primary Stages, American Theatre of Actors, and The Brighthope Company.

Bob holds a BCA from University of North Carolina at Charlotte with an emphasis in design and directing, and an MFA from Carnegie Mellon University in directing, where he also taught for three years.

Trevor O'Donnell & Co.
Marketing & Sales
Arts, Entertainment & Tourism
1859 Webster Avenue
Los Angeles, CA 90026
Telephone: 323-660-3686
Fax: 323-664-5418
trevoro@earthlink.net

www.trevorodonnell.com

Glossary

This book contains some terms that may be foreign to average readers, as well as some that may seem unusual in a book about group sales. Here is a brief glossary that describes these terms from an entertainment industry perspective:

MYTH: Myths are stories that cultures tell themselves to uphold attitudes, beliefs, values, and behaviors. Some myths reveal fundamental truths while others perpetuate undesirable or counterproductive attitudes and behaviors. In the stage entertainment industry, the stories that most people tell about group sales do the latter.

GROUP SALES: Group sales in the stage entertainment industry is a process of selling ticket inventory to volume buyers. Typically, group sales involves selling seats in blocks of 20 or more to buyers representing individuals who attend the same performance.

SALES: Sales is a process of urging customers to buy tickets. It is a proactive, rather than reactive, process that involves direct communication, such as telephone or in-person conversations. The key factor that distinguishes sales from marketing is that it relies on the use of *reason* to persuade buyers to act. Typically, sales is about learning what customers want or need, and then using that information to *persuade* them to buy.

GROUP: A group is a number of people who can be identified by their common affiliations or proximity to one another.

GROUP BUYER: A group buyer is an individual who buys tickets on behalf of groups or who agrees to motivate members of his or her group to purchase tickets.

GROUP LEADER: A group leader is a group buyer, often a senior, usually a woman, who buys group tickets for organizations with which she is affiliated. Group leaders are usually consumers, although some are quasi-professionals. This is a term that arts and entertainment professionals use incorrectly to refer to all group buyers.

BUSINESS MODEL: A business model is a description of the way a business functions. The description can be a set of guidelines to follow or a description of the way a business actually works. Business models provide overviews of the way businesses work or don't work so observers can help them work more efficiently.

BUSINESS-TO-CONSUMER: Business-to-consumer (B-to-C) is an expression used to describe businesses that sell their products directly to consumers. Stage entertainment is largely a B-to-C business because, in this business, tickets are sold primarily to consumers.

BUSINESS-TO-BUSINESS: Business-to-business (B-to-B) is an expression used to describe businesses that sell their products to other businesses. Those products may be re-sold to consumers or used to further the buyer's business objectives. Stage entertainment professionals engage in B-to-B practices when they sell tickets to businesses that, in turn, sell or distribute them to others.

BUNDLED SINGLES: Bundled singles, otherwise known as super-groups, refers to tickets that are sold individually by group ticket sellers and then reflected in the books as group sales (bundled to conform to group policies). The practice, which exploits a loophole in most group policies and procedures, gives group ticket sellers the ability to respond to demand from buyers who can't work with existing consumer ticketing systems.

ON-SALE: The on-sale period is the time established by a show's producer or presenter for making tickets available to the public. Because producers and presenters don't understand group ticket buying behavior, they often plan group on-sale periods poorly.

SIT-DOWN: This refers to when a touring show sits down for a while in a particular market. Sit-down productions run for months, whereas most touring shows run for days or weeks.

COLLATERAL: Marketing and sales materials that are printed and intended for distribution are known as collateral.

ONE-OFF: One-off refers to deals that happen once and aren't likely to happen again. We use the expression to distinguish isolated deals from those that ore ongoing or may have long-term consequences. Selling last-minute tickets to a group of visiting consumers may be considered a one-off, whereas selling tickets to a tour operator who delivers multiple groups to the same destination offers greater long-term potential.

DESTINATION: A place that travelers visit.

DESTINATION MARKETING: The act of marketing a place to travelers. This usually involves some sort of cooperative activity among those who benefit from visitor spending. Group travel is a potent market for group ticket sellers so destination marketing is important to them.

DESTINATION MARKETING ORGANIZATION: Destination marketing organizations (DMOs), as the name suggests, are organizations that market destinations. DMOs are usually cooperative entities that are run by businesses and government entities that benefit from travel spending. Convention and visitors bureaus are DMOs, as are chambers of commerce and government tourism marketing agencies.

SOME TOURISM ACRONYMS:

ABA: American Bus Association: An association of motor coach operators and group tour professionals.

ASAE: American Society of Association Executives: A trade group for association executives.

DMC: Destination management company: A business that plans local gatherings and events for remote clients.

EIBTM: European Incentive and Business Travel Marketplace: An annual trade event for incentive travel buyers.

FIT: Foreign Independent Traveler: In entertainment we say groups and single tickets. It travel and tourism, we say groups and FITs.

MICE: Meetings, incentives, conventions & events. This is an informal expression used to distinguish one family of corporate buyers from other group markets.

MPI: Meeting Professionals International: a trade association for meeting professionals.

NTA: National Tour Association: North America's largest association of group tour and package travel professionals.

OMCA: Ontario Motor Coach Association: A trade group for Canadian group travel professionals.

RSAA: Receptive Services Association of America: A trade association for receptive tour operators and their suppliers.

SITE: Society of Incentive Travel Executives: A trade association for incentive travel professionals.

SYTA: Student Youth Travel Association: a trade association of professionals who deal with student group travel.

TIA: Travel Industry Association of America: A trade group concerned with the world tourism industry as it relates to North America.

USTOA: United States Tour Operators Association: A trade group for the top package travel companies in the U.S.

For more information on these and other related organizations, visit Travel Industry Association of America at www.tia.org.